It's Giving Life

It's Giving Life

A Guide to Surviving and Thriving

GK BARRY

EBURY
SPOTLIGHT

EBURY SPOTLIGHT

UK | USA | Canada | Ireland | Australia
India | New Zealand | South Africa

Ebury Spotlight is part of the Penguin Random House group of companies
whose addresses can be found at global.penguinrandomhouse.com

Penguin Random House UK
One Embassy Gardens, 8 Viaduct Gardens, London SW11 7BW

penguin.co.uk

First published by Ebury Spotlight in 2026
1

Designed and set by seagulls.net

Printed and bound in Great Britain by Clays Ltd, Elcograf S.p.A.

The authorised representative in the EEA is Penguin Random House Ireland, Morrison Chambers, 32 Nassau Street, Dublin D02 YH68.

A CIP catalogue record for this book is available from the British Library

ISBN 9781529985627

MIX
Paper
FSC® C018179

Penguin Random House is committed to a sustainable future for our business, our readers and our planet. This book is made from Forest Stewardship Council® certified paper.

This book is dedicated to my mum and dad,
Loretta and Andrew. Not just because they raised a
skinny legend, but because everything I do is to give back
to them for all the sacrifices they made for me.

CONTENTS

Introduction

Well, well, well ...

So, guys, Mummy wrote a book.

This is quite the achievement for me considering the last time I authored anything longer than a WhatsApp message was when I did the dissertation for my master's degree. And I used ChatGPT for that. Allegedly.

But here we are and here it is. It is a thing that actually exists.

Before we jump in, I should probably tell you what this book isn't. It's not an autobiography (I'm still too fresh out the womb) or self-development guide (lol, come on now). Neither does it contain a magic formula that's going to give you the solution to surviving every plot twist life decides to throw at you.

This might shock some of you to hear, but, full disclaimer, I'm not a medical professional or a trained therapist and so none of my 'advice' – and I use the term in the loosest possible sense – should be taken as gospel.

Or even at all.

I'm not an expert on anything except my own life and, therefore, my multitude of fuck-ups, and that's what I'm going to be sharing with you here in an attempt to make all of you feel better about yourselves. In other words, I'm laying every last bit of personal humiliation out there for the greater good of humanity, which basically makes me a saint and you can thank me later.

Tragically for me, I have very little semblance of shame left to lose. The damage is already done for me and if I ever have kids, I'll have to assume a new identity and reinvent myself in another country before they learn how to google. But because we're all trying to navigate our way through life and it is *wild* out there, I wanted this book to be raw, reckless and 100 per cent unfiltered. Social media is just a snapshot of what goes on with me day to day, and I normally have to be restrained when I'm on TV because obviously I can't go on *Loose Women* and talk about body counts, cocks and chlamydia. So this has been a chance to unpack everything and dig in.

With that in mind, I'm going to give you the tea on losing my virginity, STIs, pube trauma, hangxiety, sexuality and why I became a raging lez. We'll delve into body image, dating disasters, the digital world, dealing with exes, getting revenge on the pricks who made your life hell at school and how to start caring less about the opinions of others.

I'm also going to be helping with some of your real-life dilemmas so buckle up for that because some of those situations are severely off the rails.

Expect the following pages to be full of hypocrisy, contradictions and terrible takes because I'm very much still figuring all this out myself. But if you enjoy streams of consciousness and the confessions of a semi-functioning 20-something under construction then you're in the right place.

It might not cure your entire existence, but by the time you've finished reading, I guarantee you will be at least 25 per cent hotter. So congrats in advance for that.

Let's get into it.

CHAPTER ONE

I Blame the Parents

Family drama, teenage rebellion and why I am the way I am

I'm going to introduce you to my family by way of three statements. Only two of these statements are true – see if you can work out which one is the lie.

1. My dad nearly died in a plane crash alongside a priest in an aircraft he was piloting.
2. My mum used to host boozy house parties for the prime minister and almost killed one of his security dogs.
3. My brother once dated Carol Vorderman after they met at a maths convention in Blackpool.

Put it this way: my family is not normal. I love them to pieces most of the time, but they are genuinely deranged and my whole life has been full of insane situations that have been very much caused by my parents. It's actually quite miraculous that I've turned out so mentally stable.

Let's start with my mother.

Loretta is an icon, no question. She's the life and soul of the party. After a few drinks, she has been known to be ejected from a treadmill at high speed (don't ask) before rising like Lazarus and asking for a top-up. It has to be seen to be believed.

But she is also absolutely unfiltered and therefore terrifying to be around in a group setting because whatever secret I've divulged with the instruction on pain of death that she's not to tell anyone else, one glass of Prosecco and she'll have fucked it.

Everyone in that room will know, along with her extra 10 per cent detail added for good measure.

So, while in my eyes she's the definition of a living legend, she's also very cancellable and we have to be extremely careful where we let her loose.

That woman raised me on Prosecco. When she breastfed me, it was the fizzy stuff coming out of those bad boys. And she has lived a life. She's on her third husband and speaks about weddings like they're a day out at Tesco and, honestly, I love that for her.

I know my family set-up is something that causes confusion – right from the day I was born, people would ask how my dad was Black but I was white. So, let me set the record

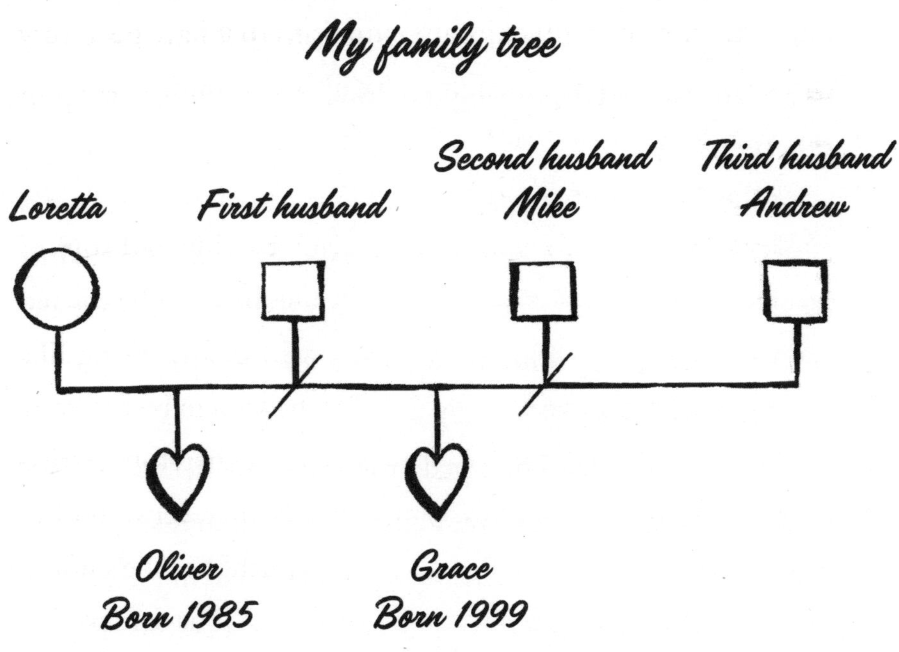

straight here. My older brother Oli is my mum's son with a different bloke. Then came my biological dad, Mike, who my mum split from when I was two, and after him there's my step-dad, Andrew, who I grew up with and also call Dad.

What can I say? I love her. We'll drive through places like Bromley or Beckenham and she'll go, 'Oh, I used to date a man from here' and then tell me what became of that relationship.

I was born in Cambridgeshire on 12 August 1999, and spent my early years living on Virgin Gorda, which is part of the British Virgin Islands. My dad (as in Andrew, husband number three) worked as a firefighter there. He's from Trinidad and we didn't move back to the UK until I was five or six which, I'll level with you, was a shock to the system. I was able to open a coconut with my bare hands, had my hair in cornrows and possessed a full-on Caribbean accent which made me sound like Sean Paul – I'd probably be done for cultural appropriation these days.

All of that made me a complete weirdo at my small, very Christian, very white school in very Christian, very white Newmarket, so I made a conscious effort to lose the accent and went the other way entirely. Within a few months I sounded like Princess Diana, RIP.

I was doing what I had to do to fit in, but I became so well spoken for a while and it was a phase I'd forgotten about until someone (thanks, Mum) dug out an old video of me which was played on *This Morning* during an interview a couple of years ago. Hearing myself talking like I should be called Bunty and quaffing Pimm's at a regatta shook me to my very core and, given how I speak now, it made me appear a total fraud to the entire nation. Another great day for me.

⚢

I might not have been around my biological dad much growing up, but he's at the centre of so many key memories because the time I did spend with him was so mental. He's a cute old man now, knocking on for 80, so I literally can't be pissed off at him for anything anymore, but after he split up from my mum, he went to live in America where he invited me to spend one Christmas. At the time he was with this crazy hardcore Republican woman (we'll call her Penny) who was best friends with Donald Trump long before he was anywhere near the presidency. Penny's previous two husbands had both mysteriously died, although we mustn't speculate.

So I'm about eight years old when I go to stay with them and this woman is certifiably mad. While I'm there, she cuts off all my hair, dresses me head to toe in Lilly Pulitzer (think pastel, patterned Palm Beach country club) and on Christmas Day she gives me a Barbie doll, possibly in an attempt to replace the rabbit teddy, Rabbie Williams, that I carried everywhere and still sleep with today. Don't judge.

Whatever the reason, I wasn't ever a Barbie kind of girl so it was clear Penny really didn't know me at all. She was also massively insecure and she'd say things like, 'Urgh, you love your mom more than me!' which I obviously did because my mum was my actual mum.

Dad eventually got kicked out of America after forgetting to renew his visa. He'd tried to get back in but they said, 'Absolutely not,' so he returned home to live in the UK.

Is this a lot? It feels like it might be.

Things my family did that made me consider putting myself up for adoption*

- Slow-cooked dinners. I wouldn't wish them on anyone. I'd come home from a really stressful day at school, my mum would tell me it was slow-cooked beef for dinner and it would send me into oblivion.
- Watching my grandma's dentures move around her mouth while she ate her dinner. To this day, I can't eat lamb.
- Being force-fed *Strictly Come Dancing*. Hell.
- My mum cleaning the house as if the Queen was coming for dinner, something that triggered my entire being.
- Going on holiday as an only child. On my own with no phone signal while my parents got pissed. Dreadful times.

* But, upon reflection, were no big deal.

- My parents' annual house party which wasn't for the weak. My mum and her school friends would just get obliterated and it was a tough watch, ngl.
- Going shopping with my dad, who as a joke would say, 'Why are you following me? Stop following me. Who are you? What are you doing?' And because he's Black and I'm white and we didn't look like father and daughter, everyone would think I was the weirdo.
- My mum doing impressions of Austin Powers and saying, 'Yeah, baby' in social situations which still makes my skin crawl now.

Growing up, me and my mum would bicker all the time. I reckon the menopause had a significant part to play in that and I don't want to say anything out of turn, but fuck me, for about two years the woman was unhinged.

I wasn't allowed to wear tracksuits because they were 'too big' for the washing machine and 'too difficult' to dry, and everything I did seemed to anger her. There were times when we were arguing constantly, but as we lived in the middle of nowhere it wasn't like I could storm off. Where would I go? The local field?

I was also capable of being a right mouthy bitch, trapped in a moody fog of hormones, and so there were endless battles. I'd answer back in a way I never had the balls to do with the teachers at school which meant me and Mum were permanently at war.

We'd clash over the food she made me because her cooking was so bland and caveman. We'd argue about cleaning my room, social media, how much time I was spending on my phone (I was always on my phone), the mates I was knocking around with.

Like Gabby. Again, I've changed the name.

Gabby's parents didn't love her – her bedroom was a cupboard under the stairs, like a real-life Harry Potter – and she was allowed to do whatever she wanted because her mum and dad didn't care. Shit for Gabby, but great for me because she was absolutely feral and me and my other friend Kim got to live out all our inner savagery with her. She'd influence us to smoke rollies which made us feel sick but we did it anyway because we thought it made us look cool. We'd go and get pissed in the park, drinking Cactus Jack's topped up with Glen's Vodka, which is basically battery acid, while my mum thought we were having a wholesome girlie sleepover, unaware that I was passed out in a field at 4am.

Eventually, she cottoned on and banned me from seeing Gabby, who she said was a bad influence, but by then I could lie to my parents without blinking.

'Can you drop me off at Alice's for a sleepover?' I'd ask. The only thing was, 'Alice' never existed and for six months Mum was delivering me straight to my boyfriend's to stay the night.

If I ever have a child who does that, it'll put me into a coma.

⚢

My dad (as in my stepdad Andrew – keep up, guys) has the patience of a saint. He's had to, being married to my mum, but the two of them work together and they really do love each other.

He is fucking hilarious. He's so soft, like the soppiest man ever, and he could talk the hind leg off a donkey about anything – politics, travel, food, Formula One. If he could date Lewis Hamilton, I think he would.

He's very laid back compared to my mum – a typical Caribbean man, very nonchalant with an 'it is what it is' type approach to life. If me and Mum were ever at loggerheads, my dad would normally take her side and question why I was making life so hard, but apart from that, me and him never argued unless we were doing homework together because I didn't know what pi was. Still don't, have never needed to and I bet you haven't either so why are we doing this?

We were always messing about and one day when I was about ten, he said it would be really funny if I recorded the voicemail message to the house landline in a Jamaican accent.

'We're not here to take your call,' I said into the tape, 'but leave your name and your number and we'll get back to you … Shabba.'

We genuinely had this message for an entire YEAR and Mum had no idea until the day the vet's receptionist called us and the voicemail she left was just the sound of the whole practice screaming laughing. They'd thought they'd hung up, but the answerphone had recorded her shrieking to her colleagues to come and have a listen to this and then calling back a second time to hear it again.

My mum checked the message, heard me being a dick, went loopy and we had to change it.

So, Dad was mischievous, but my brother Oli was the worst. He's always been the loose cannon of the family, constantly in trouble and a bit like Peter Pan in that he'll probably never grow up. When I was eight or nine, he was home from university in France and told me to put my Snow White costume on, gave me a cigarette to smoke and had me racking up a line of flour while he took pictures for a photography project.

It was obviously a joke and Dad thought it was funny as fuck, but my mum went nuts.

Oli lives in New York now, still loves a party but is also very American these days. He'll call me 'dude', which is unacceptable to me and I'm like, 'Who are you even talking to?'

Somebody needs to save him, actually.

What I get from my dad

- Morals
- How to season food properly
- A strong head on my shoulders
- The ability to see the world from different points of view
- A sense of adventure
- Work ethic
- Being an overgrown kid

What I get from my mum

- Ability to work a room
- Tolerance to alcohol
- Dark humour
- One-liners
- Love of gossip
- Saying 'Ah, we do have fun' after every joke
- My awful driving. My mum needs to be taken off the roads and I 100 per cent have inherited that trait from her

Most people will grow out of not getting on with their parents. Obviously if yours are psychopathic serial killers who kept you locked in a basement then you should maybe reconsider your relationship. But if they're basically normal people trying their best, then believe it or not, it's probably you who's the arsehole.

At 16, I thought I was right about everything and my mum was out there sabotaging my life on purpose, but I can see now that most of the time I was just being a little bitch for the sake of it. It's funny how your viewpoints change as you get older. If I'd been asked back then what my mum should have done differently in bringing me up, I'd have produced a long list of her crimes, but now I think she absolutely should have done everything exactly the same.

Despite the ups and downs, we have a brilliant relationship today and in 2024 we went on holiday to Barbados as a family, the first time we'd been away together in about ten years. I'd been worried beforehand that there were going to be points where they pushed my buttons and sent me over the edge. I'm very much a 'let's do piss all and just get drunk all day long' type of person on holiday. And if we *are* going to do an activity, let's make it wine tasting.

My parents, on the other hand, want to go and explore, walk around and find a historic building or a volcano.

But we all had the best time together (thank God for alcohol, which helped) and, without getting too dramatic, it reminded me how lucky I am to have them. My mum will definitely still tell me off and we'll have one big blowout a year, usually over something she's said that she shouldn't have, but she's more like my friend these days and I've learned, accepted and even embraced that the reason we clash is because we're so similar.

That's just my mum.

Families can be complex. I know it can feel tricky when you're caught in the middle of situations that started when you were a kid or even before you existed at all. When there's history, it's sometimes difficult to form close relationships with people, but most of this stuff gets easier and less intense as you grow up and time does its thing.

So, hang in there, cut your loved ones some slack and try to avoid the drama. I'm like an ostrich these days. Head, sand, peace out.

⚢

In case you're wondering about my two truths and a lie.

My dad nearly died in a plane crash in an aircraft he was flying alongside a priest: TRUE

My biological dad flew planes for fun because he was rich. His plane was called *Rocky Wings* and one time he was flying across Cape Cod with this priest guy he knew and the engine just gave way over the ocean. He had to crash land into the water and, amazingly, both he and the priest survived. I only found out about this days later when he sent me a link to the news article along with a message, 'Was just in a plane crash. All good, though. Hope you're well.'

My mum used to hold house parties for the prime minister and nearly killed one of his security dogs: TRUE

When my mum was still with my brother's dad, he was the sort of man who always had a deal on the go which meant he had loads of rich and famous friends.

In the early nineties they lived in this massive old schoolhouse. I'm not sure how they originally formed the connection, but it was probably through being raging Tories. My mum definitely isn't a Tory anymore but back then they'd host a massive party every year for the then Conservative prime minister John Major. His team would come to the house with a load of sniffer dogs to recce the joint beforehand and make sure there were no bombs planted and it was during a routine check like this that one of the dogs found my brother's wine gums, ate the entire pack which stuck his jaw together and he had to go to the vets and get it prised apart.

My brother once dated Carol Vorderman after they met at a maths convention in Blackpool: LIE

I'm sad to report this is untrue because having Vorders as your sister-in-law would be anyone's dream scenario. Carol Vorderman at the Christmas dinner table? Are you kidding me? That would be iconic.

CHAPTER TWO

Surviving School

Bullies, social media trauma and the actual hell of prom

Things I don't miss about school

- **The horror of the girls' toilets** where I had to pray for my life every time I entered.
- **The watery pasta served in the canteen.** A sick and twisted joke.
- **Non-uniform days** and the pressure to prove that you had fashion sense and show off your skinniness at the same time. Nightmare.
- **Getting dropped off by a parent outside of school.** Kill me now.
- **The school bus.** I never actually got it myself, but I can imagine that needs to be burned to the ground.
- **GCSE drama performances.** Still psychologically damaged today.
- **End-of-term trips to Alton Towers.** My nervous system is unable to handle roller coasters so that's an absolutely not from me.
- **Assemblies, just awful.** I did not consent to this.
- **Being on my period.** Tampons scared the hell out of me until I was 23, so I used sanitary towels which meant having to take a dramatic cough as I ripped the pad off my knickers to conceal the fact I was on from anyone else in the toilets.

- **Maths.** To this day I don't even know how to read a 24-hour clock.
- **Pervy PE teachers.** Every school has one. Having said that, I was so bad at sport that I was put in the group who couldn't run, throw or jump to save their lives and no one was getting perved on there.
- **PE in general.** I can't cope with why we have to do sports if we don't want to. And why am I wearing shorts when the teacher is in a fleece?
- **Sports day.** Ban it. (Are you noticing a theme?)
- **The smell.** I think I'd vomit if I walked into a school now and the familiar aroma of roast beef, puberty and BO was to hit me. It would be like going back to Vietnam.

I hated every single sorry second of school life.

OK, I enjoyed fancying boys and the cheap thrill of having the one I liked brush past me in the dinner hall. But apart from that, I'd say going there every day was worse than an actual living hell.

It didn't help that I looked like the Slender Man, ridiculously skinny and freakishly tall. I had buck teeth with braces, greasy hair (which I was unashamed of) and, from my sense of humour to my taste in music, I was *weird*. Like, beyond. When everyone else was into One Direction, I was in my depressed era and listening to My Chemical Romance and Black Veil Brides. And also Jedward, so you can see that I was either suffering from a major identity crisis or severely emotionally unwell.

Probably both, actually.

There were loads of different groups at school but I didn't fit into any of them so I ended up becoming best mates with the other weird girl in my year, Kim, and we knocked around together, eating our lunch in the corridor by the electronics and woodwork room where no one else would ever go. Two 'in between' oddballs who couldn't be classed as anything, just sort of there, existing.

School groups

- **The chavs.** Hands down the best people you'll ever meet. One of them, Catherine Jones (not her real name), pierced her own tongue in the girls' toilets during a lunchbreak. Icon.
- **The nerds.** Proper gamers, definitely didn't wash, probably all billionaires and incels now.
- **The sports lot.** Lads, lads, lads with main-character energy and Justin Bieber hair. Always carried their PE kit round in a yellow JD bag and never wore the school blazer.
- **The populars.** Mostly interchangeable girls, copy-paste pretty, big messy buns with two strands down at the front.

Their uniform was black Vans, ankle socks, skintight jeans and Cath Kidston bags.

- **The lesbians.** A small group, comprising just two girls who would snog in the corner for the whole of break and lunch.
- **The music and drama kids.** Would usually merge together because they were all in the same building and wore funny ties.

My attempts to get in with the popular girls knew no bounds and I'm honestly mortified for my poor soul just thinking about that now. Trying to worm my way into their good books, I'd tell them what other people had been saying behind their backs so they basically used me for a bit of tea and I'd then fall into the trap of thinking their fake gratitude meant we were now officially friends. But outside of our form class, they wouldn't speak to or even acknowledge me and it took a shamefully long time for the penny to drop that they were just taking the piss.

I have a core memory that is so horrific I've tried everything to erase it from my brain but it simply won't leave me and I've accepted that it will haunt me for the rest of my natural life. You might remember there was this song back in the day called 'When I'm Gone' from the movie *Pitch Perfect* – Anna Kendrick (legend) sings it while keeping the beat with a plastic cup which she flips up, turns over and taps on the table in a repeating pattern. You know the one, right?

One of the popular girls, let's call her Fanny, was like, 'Tell you what, Grace, why don't we both film ourselves singing the cup song, doing all the actions and then post it on each other's Facebook walls? You post your version and then I'll post mine.'

Apologies if you're old enough to be triggered by this mention of the Facebook wall, but for those too young to know, Facebook was massively different to what it is today. Before it became overrun with AI shit and Boomers moaning about cycle lanes, everyone was on there, posting 200 pictures from their holiday and daily life updates. You didn't leave the house without telling everyone on Facebook first and your 'wall' acted like a public message board which your 'friends' could post whatever the fuck they wanted directly onto for everyone to see.

With hindsight, this was deeply problematic and is literally why we're all mentally ill now.

'Won't that be, like, really embarrassing?' I said, slightly suspicious of Fanny's motivations.

'Naaah, we should totally do it,' she replied.

So that evening, off I went and filmed myself singing 'When I'm Gone' while mastering the whole routine with my plastic cup on the kitchen surface. I think we can all agree just by looking at me that it's obvious that I can't sing. I ain't no J.Lo or Beyoncé and my turkey neck restricts me from being able to hold any kind of note, but in my mind, I was fucking great. I'd nailed this.

So, I posted the video on Fanny's wall and waited for her to post on mine.

And I waited.

I waited some more.

I had been right to be suspicious. At some point in the evening, it became clear this absolute arsehole wasn't going to post anything and, indeed, had never had any intention of doing so, but by now it was too late to save face and remove my own. It was up on her wall in all its shameful glory and everyone had seen it.

I had the piss taken out of me for years because of that and still have recurring nightmares about it.

Fanny is actually a paramedic these days, so good luck to whoever that bitch is picking up.

Things at school I was good at

- Lying
- Playing the victim to avoid getting told off
- Going home. I excelled at that
- Ummm …

Although I was never beaten up, there were a lot of side-eye intimidation and 'you can't sit with us' vibes. But you can't go up to someone and say, 'Stop giving me dirty looks,' because they'll a) deny doing it and b) tell you not to look at them.

I did once get into an unintentional fight with a girl who had been going around telling everyone I'd slept with some boy and, as a result, was now pregnant.

'My queen,' I said, approaching her in the corridor, 'why are you saying all this about me?'

'Get out my way,' she snarled.

'I won't get out your way,' I replied, 'until you tell me why you've been spreading shit about me.'

I was woefully under-prepared for what happened next.

This girl suddenly swings for me so I'm now in the position of having to physically defend myself and, given the fact I weigh about two stone, the odds are not in my favour. I launch a fist right back at her and end up hitting the wind – no connection, not even close – then I lose my balance and fall over.

Remember Miss Sexy trousers? Super skinny, super tight, gave us all yeast infections and ended up getting banned at schools up and down the country for being too slutty? Well, obviously I'm wearing a pair of those, aren't I? And as I collapse like a paper hanky to the floor, there's no way the Miss Sexys are staying in position, so I manage to expose my red frilly thong from Primark as well as half my arse to the whole of the watching corridor.

My friend Kim can bear it no longer. She steps in to scoop me up and escorts me off, my adrenaline now pumping so hard that I nearly throw up the potato ball I'd eaten shortly before the confrontation. It was not a good day to be me and I was put in isolation for that incident.

⚢

Most of the bullying I experienced happened online where the usual pricks would send a vague-sounding tweet which I'd know was about me but had no way of proving. I was once dating a boy I was obsessed with even though he had more gum than teeth, and these girls in the year above who also fancied him went out of their way to be as vile as possible to me on social media.

One of them would post stuff on Twitter like, 'When someone thinks they're slick by chatting shit ... '

She also put up a picture of a fat dead fish and said, 'This looks exactly like her.'

Of course, then I'd have to reply – you've got to back yourself, yeah? – so I'd tweet, 'lol, @ me next time.'

And then they actually would @ me and I'd have nowhere else to go after that.

Listen, I know this is petty drama and I do laugh about it now, but it was all-consuming at the time. Once, I got into a Facebook argument with someone and wrote, 'I'm so 2008 and you're so two thousand and late,' thinking everyone would think it was so profound and clever – Shakespearean, even – and not just a lyric I'd stolen from a Black Eyed Peas song.

But that person replied saying, 'Oh my God, lol, boom boom, pow,' completing the lyric I'd tried to pass off as my own and I had no option but to delete my message and then take myself off for a full-blown existential crisis in my bedroom. It transpired that Black Eyed Peas (a band I genuinely thought my dad had brought over from the Caribbean and who no one would have heard of) were played on a fairly regular basis on Kiss, Radio 1 and Capital.

I wish now that I'd cared less. It's easy to say that when you're a bit older but at school, that whole environment feels like the be-all and end-all of your entire life and if you can't make yourself liked by these people then you might as well crawl under a rock and give up.

But the thing is, when you leave school, none of this matters. Within minutes of walking away from that trauma academy for good, it's so irrelevant and, trust me on this, it's fine to wipe that period from your history completely. With all due respect, the people whose shit didn't stink at school, that's where they peak. You could go back to your hometown in 30 years' time and they will still be sat in the same pub having the same conversations and reminiscing about their old school days. They are the least interesting people in the world.

A case in point. There was a popular boy who I'll be generous to here and won't name, but he was probably the hottest guy in the year. The generational pull, brilliant at sport, tall, attractive, smart and he knew it. He was also a nasty piece of work and would name-call, take the piss in a really vicious way and get his kicks from stirring the pot if there were ever any girl-on-girl fall-outs.

I saw him in a pub a few years back with a load of other boys from school and they came over to apologise to me for behaving like dicks and I was pleased to note that they all have dad bods and coke addictions now. Natural consequences.

What's funniest to me is that the very same bellends who gave me the most shit at school have been the ones who have tried to lodge themselves firmly up my arse since I started getting a bit of a public profile. A couple of years ago, bitch-in-chief of the populars messaged me like, 'You are smashing it, babe, so proud of you!'

And because I'm so lame, I messaged her back and said thank you. I *thanked* her!

I've developed a bit more of a spine since then and if she got in touch now, I wouldn't say thank you.

I'd say, 'I can't believe you've just had the balls to message me after making my life hell for so many years. Oh, and your breath smells like gone-off shrimp and I hate you. Get fucked.'

And that, my friends, is what you call growth.

How to deal with pricks in school

- Imagine them in ten years' time being really ugly, boring and unsuccessful because, mark my words, that's what they'll be.
- Don't try and respond with a smart answer; they're not worth the effort and if you're like me, you'll only fumble it and give them another three months of ammunition.
- Take the high road and ignore it. That'll send them insane.

- If you're built like me, avoid any physical confrontation at all costs. It will only end in public humiliation and you may have to emigrate as a result.

I was a pathological liar at school. Not about deep things (I'm not a sociopath) but random stuff for absolutely no reason. It sort of became the only hobby I had.

'Yeah, so I've got a boyfriend who lives in the States. His name's Jeremiah.' That kind of stuff.

I'd lie profusely about fake boyfriends, fictional friends, family members, things that other people had (hadn't) said to me, but it would often come and bite me on the arse and I'd have to back down immediately because I had no defence.

Me: 'You'll never guess what Louisa told me ... '

Cut to Louisa catching wind of my lie.

Louisa: 'Grace, I literally didn't say that to you.'

A pause.

Me: 'Yeah, you're absolutely right, Louisa. You didn't say that to me at all.'

I lied about starting my periods for a whole year before I actually did. That meant when they started for real in Year 9, I couldn't share it with anyone, even though it was the beginning of hell for me because I suffered from heavy bleeds until I went on the pill.

And what a day that was, by the way. My mum accompanied me to the doctor's surgery and spoke for me the whole time.

'Are you sure you want to go on the contraceptive pill?' the GP asked me.

I looked at my mum.

'Yes, she does,' she replied.

'But do *you* want it, Grace?' he addressed me again. I'm sure he thought I was being trafficked.

Anyway, lying was probably my way of getting attention, of trying to impress people so they'd think I was cool and it gave me something to talk about because I had literally no chat. My brother Oli is 15 years older than me, so I was more or less an only child and we lived in the middle of nowhere where there were no other kids. All our neighbours had cataracts. So I'd come into school and make up these fake stories to cover up the fact that I'd actually spent my weekend bored out of my brain and doing fuck all.

To be fair, I wasn't doing much more than that when I was *in* school and genuinely thought I was going to have to be a stripper when I left. I had zero skills in anything and didn't have the confidence to ask the teacher if I didn't understand something in a lesson, which was often.

And because the message was constantly hammered home that 'if you don't get good GCSEs, you're never going to work, your life will be an unholy mess and you might as well die,' whoring myself around a metal pole was the only career plan that made sense.

I was in the bottom set for every subject. The other kids in there with me, God love 'em, all had dyslexia, chronic ADHD and other very good reasons for struggling with the work, whereas I was just thick as shit and every school report said the same thing – doesn't listen, talks too much, is on her way to failing, an overall lost cause. The teachers just gave up on me.

I hated science, hated maths, hated graphics. I was all right at English but even creative subjects like drama I couldn't handle because there was no way I was getting up to degrade myself by acting out improv sketches in front of people who already didn't like me.

Of all the teachers there was only one I liked, Miss Knight, aka the BFG on account of her being about six foot eight tall. She taught electronics, had proper ginger hair that made her look like Merida from *Brave* and was this boss bitch who took no shit, especially from the boys. I think she recognised I was a bit odd which is why she had a soft spot for me – I was the only girl in that class because my parents had forced me to take it for GCSE on the basis that 'it'll look good on your CV, Grace'.

Er, not when you get an E it won't.

But apart from Miss Knight, I wished death to absolutely every teacher in that godforsaken school. I tried to skive lessons, heading down to the big smoking tree at the bottom of the field where it was just me and all the ADHD kids who couldn't sit still. Or I'd bunk off PE to walk round town aimlessly instead.

I got caught once, on the day of my drama GCSE practical which was to be a performance in front of the examiners. I'd been given the very appropriate role of Death, a part that required me to be dressed as a skeleton, all in black and with my face painted white.

The head pulled me to the side after the lesson I hadn't been in.

'Grace Keeling. Were you smoking behind the drama block?'

'No, sir. It wasn't me. I literally don't know why you'd say that.'

'That's strange, Grace. Because you are the only person in the entire school who is dressed as a skeleton.'

'That's valid, sir.'

In the end, I only passed two GCSEs – English and drama – and they were both a C so I wasn't exactly setting the world alight there either. I hadn't helped myself, doing next to no study for any of those exams because I had no idea how to revise. I didn't have the attention span or the inclination to sit there shagging a textbook when I could have been pissing about on social media instead.

Some things never change, right?

Things I was doing when I should have been revising for my GCSEs

- Arguing with people on Facebook.
- Playing *Animal Crossing* on the Nintendo.
- Sexy dancing in front of the mirror to the Pussycat Dolls.

- Worrying about imminent death.
- Worrying about Justin Bieber getting a girlfriend.
- Worrying about the shaving rash on my fanny (it was an absolute tragedy down there until I was 20).
- Sitting on my bed staring into space.
- Posting deep and meaningful 'no one gets me' black-and-white images to my really depressing Tumblr, hoping everyone would see it and be like, 'My God, she's so cool and sad.'

Before I escaped completely, there was one final humiliation to endure: the end-of-year prom. A fully fledged emotional trauma that needs to get in the sea. Who's with me?

I knew I needed a date, so I pretended to like this Jesus boy and even faked being religious just so he would go to the prom with me. Say what you like about me, guys, but if I'm going to commit to a cause, I don't do it in a half-arsed way.

I will go all out.

So I bought a Bible – a pink one – and highlighted all the notable passages in order to impress everyone with my extensive psalm knowledge at the Christian youth club I'd joined on Friday evenings.

I even went as far as getting baptised and it was at this point my poor mum and dad thought, quite reasonably, that I was having a full mental breakdown. But since they're generally quite supportive of my breakdowns, they came along to the church and watched all this play out in real time. I'd assumed that when I went under the water to be blessed into the church, the real-life God would make himself known to me, welcome me to the community and rubber-stamp my free entry to heaven but funnily enough that didn't happen, which was disappointing.

I persevered with the madness nonetheless and shortly afterwards attended a three-day Jesus Camp which, I have to say, was an actual cult. Here's me, naively thinking that since we were all young and on a camping trip together, maybe we'd all get a bit pissed. It would be as if we were living our best lives at Glastonbury. But there wasn't a drop of alcohol to be found, not anywhere.

Believe me, I looked.

Instead, there was a massive God tent where we'd all gather at night to sing happy-clappy 'Jesus loves you' bangers before some random guy asked all the young girls to stand up and publicly declare they were going to wait until marriage to have sex.

Of all the insanity, this was the point where I thought, *Now, hold on a minute. I don't wanna be rude but …*

I realised there could be no future for me here and me and the church would have to part ways, but I had to keep up the act for a few more months because I needed to go to the school prom with Jesus boy. That had been the whole point of this exercise all along.

I've actually blocked out most of prom night itself because of PTSD, but I wore a *My Big Fat Gypsy Wedding*-style pink dress – pathetically, Kim got the exact same one except hers was blue. We had both thought 'more is more' was the 'in' look – neither of us got the memo that everyone else was going classy and demure and so there we were in these jump-scare dresses, sticking out like a pair of tragic pink and blue sore thumbs all night.

To make matters worse, I'd had a spray tan plus my hair and makeup done by a woman who should have had her licence revoked. The colour of my body didn't match my face which was still so pale that I looked like a Victorian waif.

The whole night was weird vibes. It was creepy boys and people trying joints for the first time – I did a toke, but was too scared to inhale so just held it in my mouth instead (lol, that'll probably come back to haunt me in ten years' time) before exhaling and pretending to choke, like 'Whoa, that was crazy ... '

Once the main event had finished, there was 'after prom' where different people had various house parties, but obviously me and Kim didn't get invited to any of them. We ended up at a rejects' gathering with about four other people and then I got my dad to pick me up at 10pm, drunk on Echo Falls wine. So blessed.

As soon as prom was over, I broke up with Jesus boy and quit the church. Thank you, nice to meet you all, goodbye, see you in heaven. With everything I've done in my life since, I'd probably spontaneously burst into flames if I set foot in a church now while all the lesbians from history dragged me down to hell.

How to make it through your prom

- The most exciting part is getting out the car and having your pictures taken – enjoy that bit.
- Know that you are going to have way better nights out than this. Inside there's a photobooth and some fruit squash. That's it.
- Wear an outfit you like and which complements your shape, not what you think is on trend. Every single prom dress that has been 'on trend' I promise looks hideous in ten years' time.
- Don't go.

Queens, wait till you hear this: weird is good. I honestly don't know a single successful person today who wasn't weird as a teenager – the most creative minds are born out of having a shitty time at school and if I'd sailed through Years 7 to 11 as one of the populars, I don't think I'd be doing what I do now.

When I was younger, my biological dad who has loads of money had offered me the chance to be privately educated. I visited this posh school to have a look round, but all the girls there were wearing ankle-length green skirts and I thought, 'Nah, this ain't for me. I have to show a bit of leg.'

I honestly believe if I'd gone there, I wouldn't have been funny. No offence, I know I'm generalising here, but at private school, people tend to be from the same walk of life and none of them are really struggling to get by. State school was more rough and ready, like a bootcamp for all the survival skills you'll ever need; it gave me a bit of character and definitely shaped my humour. So I'm thankful for that, and even though I had to put up with the toxic shits who also went there, perspective and hindsight go hand in hand and I can see now there were plenty of poor bastards who had it way worse than me.

In no particular order:

- The girl who was off for three days while the rumour went round that she was ill from putting Whiskas on her fanny and getting her cat to lick it out. It was a complete and utter fabrication but it stayed with her until she left school and probably ruined her life. I mean, I'm still talking about it now.
- The loner boy who, if we were in America, would definitely have been a school shooter.
- The two lesbians because there were no lesbians back then and that must have been rough.

- Any closeted gay male, like my friend who loved Nicki Minaj and wore crop tops but had to pretend he was straight. This was the countryside, where gay people didn't exist.
- The girl who shagged a guy in the school forest which was right next to and in full sight of a primary school. There was no coming back from that.
- The nerds. They were so invisible at school which I can see is both a blessing and a curse, but I bet it sucked for them.

Due to the fact I barely had a GCSE to my name, post-school I ended up at Cambridge Reject College. Obviously it wasn't really called that, but everyone knew it as such because none of us who went there had enough brain cells to go anywhere else.

I remember going along for the open day and telling the woman behind the desk that I wanted to do Level 3 BTEC in media then go to uni and she looked down at my GCSE results, let out a loud snort and said no chance. She told me I was going to have to start at Level 2, do that for a year and then move on to Level 3 for another two years before any university let me within a mile radius of their campus.

And when I heard that, I burst into tears in front of this woman who had just told me I'd screwed up my life and was now just sat there, really awkwardly.

'This is what you get when you don't revise, Grace,' said my mum, unhelpfully.

'Now really isn't the time, Mum.'

There was no other choice. I'd have to start at the bottom and work my way up which, to my credit, I did and, hallelujah, I made it to uni in the end. This isn't me advising anyone to copy my example of not trying at all because it'll work out regardless – the truth is, I had to work ten times harder after leaving school to make it up and I wouldn't want that for anyone.

But what I will say is that your exam results now don't need to define the rest of your life. Yeah, they matter in that moment but *only* for that moment and they don't determine what you're capable of – they don't measure your creativity and they don't dictate your worth.

It pretty much goes without saying, though, that when it came to leaving school for good, I couldn't get out of that hellhole fast enough. I might not have broken into anything resembling a sprint or even a light jog for that matter, but it was fast for me.

A legend had left the building.

CHAPTER THREE

Body Language

Boobs, bums and bringing back the bush

Things I have told myself about my body ...

1. 'People are going to look at my non-existent arse and think I have a deformity.'
2. 'My fanny is abnormal because it's not shaped like a credit card slot.'
3. 'I can't take my top off, because everyone will think I'm a boy.'
4. 'My hair is so tragic people will think I'm Rod Stewart from behind.'
5. 'My ears are out of proportion to my massive head and skinny body; none of me makes sense.'
6. 'I have the biggest nose in the history of mankind.'
7. 'These hip dips are disgusting, I must therefore filter the fuck out of them so nobody ever knows they exist.'
8. 'My posture makes me look like a severely depressed prawn.'

... versus the truth

1. Hereditary, nothing I can do about it – not even four-times daily glute workouts are going to give me a hint of a cheek (I've tried).
2. Only about 1 per cent of women have that pornified nipped and tucked vagina, the rest of us are out here making the best of it with our kebabs.
3. Small tits for the win. Life is so much easier boob-free.
4. That's what you get for over-bleaching it. Just thank Jesus for your glam team and extensions.
5. Literally no one has ever commented on my ears. I'd say they're pretty average ears and totally in proportion.
6. Don't even really notice it now and I don't even think it's that big.
7. I can't change my skeleton so that's not worth caring about.
8. Fair enough, that one is accurate.

Body image is a minefield for me. I'll be honest, I'm still navigating it so don't look to me for the answers, but I do have a slightly better grip on the whole thing these days than I have done in the past.

I've always been very conscious of my body, weight, shape etc. and at school I wanted nothing more than to be a skinny legend. Slag me if you like, but that was my priority, however misguided. This was the early 2010s when the extremely thin look was very much in and at my school it seemed almost mandatory to have an eating disorder.

I think we're all better at recognising fucked up attitudes towards body image now but Year 11 was apocalyptic. All the girls just started wasting away, dropping pounds like there was no tomorrow. Eating disorders, sadly, were aspirational and I got #influenced, starting off by skipping school dinners until my mum checked the balance on the account, saw there was nothing being spent and pulled me up on it.

After that, I started buying a panini but giving it to my friend, which meant she was having two lunches a day and went the opposite way.

The only flaw in my plan was that when I got home, I'd be so ravenous that I'd devour the entire contents of the fridge, which completely defeated all the painstaking work of depriving myself over the previous eight hours. So while I wouldn't say I ever developed an eating disorder, I did find myself trapped in a pretty dysfunctional relationship with food and to this day I can be weird about it. Food is the only thing that can send me into a blind rage and if there's been a mess-up with a takeaway order or something doesn't taste as I thought it would, then I will be vicious and it will ruin my day. Not me getting too deep on this, but I do wonder if that could all be linked.

There was body pressure everywhere, including at home where, like many, I was raised by an almond mum.* Mum was even skinnier than me and she was a runner – that woman was running all over the place, all the time. She'd eat a lettuce leaf for dinner and maybe an almond if she was treating herself. But she was a product of the culture, too. Even now she'll only have a boiled egg for lunch, so I grew up with the idea that eating in this way was somehow normal and it has definitely seeped into my own habits.

I was surrounded by people who'd watch whoever was on the telly and pick them apart, whether it was for their 'knocked knees' or being 'the size of a house', so it was drilled into me that people were always watching and critiquing. Just remember, when anyone tries to reassure you that 'people aren't looking at you, nobody's judging you' – it's not true.

⚢

* **almond mum** (***noun***) Will eat six almonds in place of a meal, believes hunger is a mindset, sees thinness as the default goal, obsessed with diet culture, tortured by internalised fatphobia, passes on own food guilt to her kids, constant talk of calories and 'being good', most likely to say, 'I've already eaten.' (She has not.)

I was constantly comparing myself to the other girls in my year as well as various female celebrities like Paris Hilton and Cara Delevingne. The questionable-at-best Victoria's Secret Fashion Show was the pinnacle of my year and I thought all the models were incredible because that was *exactly* what I wanted to look like. Golden tans, toned stomachs, big hair, skin to die for, tits that weren't too big but still gave them a decent cleavage and so skinny it looked as if every bit of air conditioning in the building needed switching off else they'd blow away.

The thing is, I was naturally extremely thin as a teenager so my actual weight was never an issue, but I was crippled with self-consciousness about it anyway and everything else besides. My tallness, my freckled legs (my mum's ginger and she passed that on to me), the absence of any sign of hips or a waist.

And that's before I've even got on to my flat-as-a-pancake arse.

Basically, I just have a long back, like the Peperami man. There's not even a fold to differentiate between the top of my leg and the bottom of my bum and at school I was frequently questioned on the whereabouts of my backside. The very trauma of that runs so deep that even now I tend to take the lead on it before anyone else gets the chance, and when I enter a room the first thing I'll say isn't 'hello,' it's 'yes, I know I have no arse, nice to meet you.' Just to make sure they don't have any leverage.

On my first tour with my *Saving Grace* podcast back in 2023, I was at a meet-and-greet in Birmingham and a girl came up to me.

'My boyfriend fancies you,' she said.

I jokingly feigned embarrassment and replied, 'Oh no!'

And then she said, 'Yeah, dunno why. Your arse is really flat.'

Wow. The audacity.

For a split second I considered picking out something about her physical appearance as a comeback because there was plenty to choose from, but I thought that might get me cancelled so instead I just said, 'You're right, it is. Thank you for coming along, do you want a picture?'

We took the photo, she moved on to continue with her day and left me in an actual quarter-life crisis. What a great first experience of meeting the general public that was.

Cosmetic surgery I've considered but ruled out

Labiaplasty (designer vagina)

Why not: I have an irrational fear that I won't wake up from the anaesthetic and imagine the embarrassment of having everyone know that you died while getting a glow-up on your vadge. Also, I fear I would suffer separation anxiety from my flaps.

Brazilian bum lift (BBL)

Why not: I had no money when I was seriously thinking about this, thank God, otherwise I'd be rocking about with a mutant arse right now and probably unable to sit down without the aid of a rubber ring. Imagine a future where care homes are full of old people whose BBLs have migrated south over the years and are now drooping down to the backs of their knees. What a world.

Buttock fillers

Why not: I heard a story about a woman who had them and nearly died of sepsis and so thought I should probably pass. If there's a high chance of death or serious injury on anything then I need to say no because I know for a fact that will be me. And I don't have time to get sepsis when I'm doing *Loose Women* on Friday.

Lip filler

Why not: My parents would whoop me. No other reason. Thinking about their reaction has stopped me from getting a lot of things done so I'm very grateful because none of this would have ended well for me, I feel sure of that.

I get messages on the daily from cosmetic surgeons or aesthetics clinics, sliding into my DMs offering me various procedures for free.

My first thought is, 'How rude.'

And my second is that if this had been a few years ago when I was 19 or 20 and clueless, I would have gone for it. Of course I would. Like a lot of people, I would have found the temptation too hard to resist because if my arse was M.I.A. then so were my boobs. For years I employed a strict policy of 'top on and lights off' in the bedroom, even when I first met Ella, my now-girlfriend and undisputed love of my life. It took me a long time to liberate the tits.

At school, I only had nipples; there wasn't so much as a pec to be seen. All the girls in my year were wearing those Primark push-up bras, but I had nothing to push up, so I'd stuff my bras with socks which wasn't a foolproof plan by any means.

My mum, God bless her, has massive milkers and so I assumed I'd get them too. We're alike in every other way – the ginger skin and flat arse are both courtesy of Loretta – so I figured my boobs would follow suit and took heart from the hope that one day I would have a rack to be proud of.

It never happened. I did eventually sprout a couple of mini mounds, but not until I was 21 and they didn't grow any bigger than the cusp of a C-cup. However, I'm actually very happy with them now – they are compact, travel-sized and efficient, and big boobs are great for those who are #blessed with them but aren't nearly as popular as they used to be. Women are queuing up to get their implants removed, aren't they? Which shows that body trends come and go and what's seen as the 'ideal' one year will be something else the next.

Whatever shape you are, it will be the on-trend aesthetic at some point, so my advice is not to bother attempting to keep up with others. If you set out to try and change yourself, by the time you get there, everyone else will have moved on.

The cycle of body trends

Skinny minnies/heroin chic (my time to shine)

Kim Kardashian and the BBL (hated everything about this era but that was all out of blind jealousy)

Strong and sporty (a truly awful time for me. Thank God that's over)

Back to skinny minnies (thanks, Ozempic)

This isn't me moaning, but one of the problems with having a public profile is that it comes with people commenting on the way you look. I went up a couple of dress sizes a few years ago and everyone told me about it, presumably in case I hadn't noticed myself, which was thoughtful of them.

I'd gained the weight from eating shit, drinking too much and being in a doomed relationship, but the critical tipping point came when I went to the 2023 Capital Summertime Ball in a too-small dress that made me look like a joint of pork tied up with string. The photos from that night were a reality check for me.

The first thing I did was dump the boyfriend because I wasn't going to be a skinny legend again while he was still on the scene with his cheeseboards and chorizo pasta. Don't come at me for this – I'm well aware that I've never been overweight – but I was unhappy with where I was and what I looked like and the simple truth is, I like being thin.

There, I said what I said.

I went hell for leather to lose the weight I'd put on and ended up taking it too far, becoming so thin that my mum staged an intervention, making it clear to my management that everyone needed to get me to eat more. I've got a healthier approach now but when I'm at an event, I still want to be the skinniest person there – it's almost like a competition in my head, maybe because I don't feel in control of anything except that.

The funny thing was, when I lost weight, the same people who'd been telling me I'd put it on were now accusing me of being on Ozempic and calling me a bad role model. Guys, I'm shit scared of needles and there is no way I could inject anything into myself, so heroin dealers needn't bother knocking on my door either.

Don't get me wrong, there are people who have been crying out for a weight-loss solution and they've absolutely smashed it out the park and look amazing. But once you start on these jabs, it seems hard to stop. I know someone who's been on them for about three years and although she looks great, she can't come off them because she's terrified of piling everything back on.

It's like a crack epidemic. No one eats anything anymore, it's just vapes and Diet Cokes all round. And who knows where we'll be in a few years' time … we used to think cigarettes were fine before they said, 'Oh, by the way, you're all going to die of cancer. Soz.'

Each to their own – your life, your body, your rules. I guess my biggest issue with the jabs is the people in the public eye who are blatantly using them but not being transparent about it.

I'm not saying anyone owes people an explanation. You do you, babe. However, if you talk about your weight on socials and claim you've dropped three stone by going to Pilates twice a week and drinking flat tummy tea when the truth is you're injecting yourself with a pen, then that's pretty dishonest and gives other people false hope.

So, queens, please. Can we not?

Bikini lines through the ages

- **Olden days (aka 1960s and 1970s):** full-on forest, completely unbothered, not even a tidy-up trim
- **1990s:** The Triangle, neatly pruned to ensure no spiders' legs
- **2000s:** The Brazilian, the landing strip
- **2010s:** The Hollywood, everything off, bald and bold

Apologies if this gives anyone the ick, but body hair has entered the chat. We're going there.

I'm all for pube positivity, but I will not have them on show. I was doing a TV ad for a razor company recently and part of the job was to demonstrate how to use their new pubic shaver. It was strictly pants on, but they wanted me to hoik a leg up and shave my actual bikini line. Guys, I'm game for most things, but being on telly with your pubes out is outrageous to me and I'm afraid that is where I had to draw the line.

To be honest, my history with body hair is a whole trauma subplot and the day my mum finally allowed me to shave my legs was one of the greatest of my life. Up until then I'd been hopping about like the Gruffalo because when puberty struck, I'd also developed abnormally hairy arms, something I'm still afflicted by, sadly for me.

I could probably live shirtless and never feel the cold.

This boy at school, we'll call him Dick for argument's sake, once caught sight of my unsleeved arm and said in front of the whole class, 'Oh my God, Grace, you literally look like a gorilla.'

Dick by name, dick by nature. But Dick was right. I scanned the other girls in my class and saw their smooth, entirely hairless arms and realised that it was time to reach for the razor. I've shaved them regularly ever since.

There's a TikToker I love called Maddie Jepson (@maddie gracejepson) who is very pro arm hair – she gets comments about hers all the time, but she couldn't give less of a fuck and I wish I could be more like her. But I'm not and so I'll continue to whip everything off – arms, legs, pits and fanny – although

I would definitely get behind a campaign to Bring Back the Bush purely to save myself from the sheer horror of waxing. I get stripped down there by my girlfriend's sister (I know that's weird) every month or so and the pain never gets any easier. For several days beforehand I have to mentally prepare for the hell awaiting me and yes, I feel great afterwards, like me and my prepubescent vagina could take on the world. But why are we doing that to ourselves?

We need a feminist uprising. If we can eradicate skinny jeans from this earth, we can surely bring back the bush.

Bring Back the Bush: a campaign plan

1. Appoint Denise Welch and Princess Kate to front it. Name me a better duo. I'll wait.

2. Pay every female TikToker to come on board and grow their bush. People are very easily led these days so I feel this would kickstart the trend.

3. Plant stickers of illustrations of hairy bushes on high streets across the UK to get people talking.

4. Post a massive billboard of me and all the girlies (including Denise and Princess Kate) with our hairy fannies topiaried like hedgerow to spell out 'BRING BACK THE BUSH' plus a hashtag.

5. Launch a version of OnlyFans called OnlyBush and you can only go on there if you create content with untamed, big, beautiful bushes.

6. Problem solved and we all run about in a wonderful overgrown utopia.

Things about my body I actually like

- My legs because they're quite long. I'm happy to get them out now, freckles and all.
- My boobs. They're small, pierced and perfectly formed.
- My toes are perhaps my greatest asset. I have an enviable score on Wiki Feet and still have all my toenails, which seems to be more than the majority of people.
- My arsehole isn't very hairy and I do feel #blessed because of that.

Being in a secure, happy relationship has worked wonders for my body confidence because if I know Ella finds me attractive no matter what, why should I worry about what anyone else thinks? If I ever moan about my pancake backside to her, she doesn't know what I'm going on about because she loves every bit of me and thinks I look great all the time.

But I struggle to believe anyone is 100 per cent happy with their body – surely it's only human to have something we would change about ourselves if we were handed a magic wand? However, I promise that you will never look as good as you do now. You have the best arse today you're ever going to have. We're all going to look like saggy sacks of shit when we get old and one day when you're 84, you'll look back at pictures of yourself and wonder what you were so worried about.

I wish I could go back to my 16-year-old self and tell her to get her fucking legs out.

I'm not saying I love myself, but I am getting better at caring less and I'm becoming more willing to step out of my body comfort zone. For instance, on a cover shoot recently, the styling brief for one of the shots was topless and a pair of tights. My boobs would be covered by a prop, but I would have to be out there in the studio pretty much as naked as the day I was born.

At first, I was like, 'You are taking the piss.'

Me? Doing a sexy pic for a magazine? Who do I think I am?

But I'm not one to kick up a fuss, so I got myself together and, consoled by the thought of the post-production airbrush, I went for it. The images were great and in the unlikely scenario that I ever do have kids and grandkids, I can show them that picture and say, 'Nana was a hot piece of shit once. Children, please do see me as a piece of meat there because I looked amazing.'

If you're healthy, you feel good in yourself and your body is doing what it needs to do for you, then it is perfect just as it is.

Embrace it and be kinder to yourself.

There really is more to life than the size of your arse.

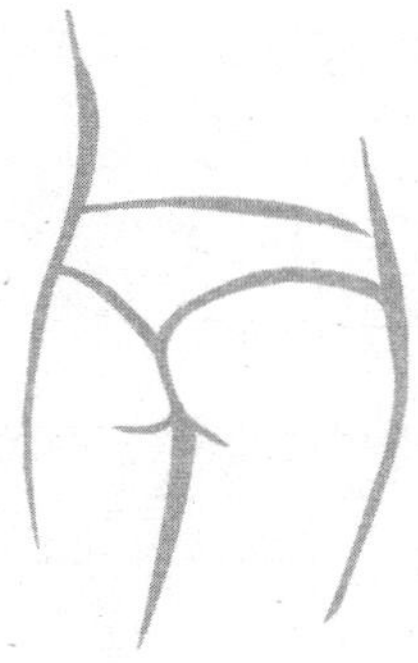

CHAPTER FOUR

Death by Hangxiety

The causes, the cures and why I'll never learn my lesson

> **hangxiety** (***noun***) A deeply spiritual state of being that develops the morning after a particularly feral night out, when the brain decides to choose violence over inner peace. Think monstrous hangover with a side order of spiral for good measure. Duration: Anything from a few hours to several days, although peak 'I need to emigrate to a remote cottage in the arse end of nowhere' energy tends to subside by the afternoon so hang in there, hun.

My first experience of hangxiety came when I was just 14 and followed an evening out drinking in the park. That night was a big deal for me because the populars had invited me to one of their field parties for the first time. And, so it turned out, the last.

I was wearing – and this is key to the living nightmare that was about to unfold – a simple pair of black cotton leggings. That was my standard look back then. Black leggings with everything, every day – an entirely inoffensive item of clothing, you might assume.

But you would assume wrong.

There I was, living my best life, drinking Cactus Jack's straight from a bottle, thinking I'd finally made it in with the clique, all while blissfully unaware that my pubes were poking out through the crotch of my leggings. At that age, I hadn't started shaving or even trimming my bush so it was like the

1970s down there and a cluster of strands had managed to find their way through the fabric.

The next day, this boy, who we'll call Ryan, put it round everyone, asking if they'd seen my pubes in the park. And guess what? They all had.

I tried to counter this narrative by claiming what they'd seen were *actually* just stray threads of elastic from my leggings, but not only was this a futile plan, it was also a lie. I knew very well that it had been my full-on pubes and so did everyone else.

The news spread like wildfire around the school and sent me into the void. I was malfunctioning at this point and this was made all the worse by the lingering taste of blue raspberry schnapps in my mouth. To this very day, it is the worst hangxiety I've known and I've kept that whole story in the depths of my soul ever since. I'm still constantly retraumatised by it.

I never wore cotton leggings again and if I happen to see them on the rail in Primark, I'm overwhelmed with chronic PTSD and have to exit the building with immediate effect.

The hangxiety timeline

- **7am:** Wake and sit up in bed like you're in *The Exorcist* with the driest throat known to man.
- **7.01am:** Try to remember when you went to bed or how you got there. Realise this is pointless as the answers

are lost to the black hole of what went down the previous night.

- **7.03am:** Reach for your phone to see if you've posted anything on your stories. If you haven't – amazing, you've cleared the first hurdle. If you have, then this is the start of a long day for you, my friend.
- **7.04am:** Delete any Insta story immediately without even watching. What you don't know can't hurt you.
- **7.10am:** Have a Lucozade.
- **7.15am:** Start trying to piece together the night, like the world's most horrific jigsaw puzzle.

  You only remember snippets of conversations but those snippets tell you that you definitely overshared and almost certainly mortally offended someone.
- **7.20am:** Oh fuck, you fell over, didn't you?
- **7.22am:** The dancing. Jesus Christ, the dancing. Who gave you permission to dance like that?
- **7.24am:** Yep, you thought you were Megan Fox, didn't you? Walking round like you were the head honcho.
- **7.25am:** The real spiralling begins. Why did you say that? Does everyone hate you? People are never going to speak to you again. Why did you share a toilet with someone when you have a bush? Did your breath stink when you

were talking to people? Why didn't you even think to have a bit of chewing gum when you were eight Jägerbombs deep?

- **7.26am:** Also, you feel sick and this is not helping the current situation.
- **8am:** OK, you're now officially a ball of TV static.
- **8.15am:** Fucking hell, someone is typing on the group chat. You are not ready for this.
- **8.17am:** The debrief of the night before begins. Brace yourself because things are about to get a whole lot worse and there will be no rest until around 8pm when you've crawled your way out of the mud. Even then The Fear will remain strong.

By day two I'm usually able to get going with my day although approximately every hour, boom, a memory of something I've said or done will pop into my head. My stomach will drop to the floor and I literally have to die on the spot.

When that happens, I have been known to slap myself around the face, as if I've got some sort of disorder, just to get the thoughts out of my brain.

After a second night's sleep, things have normally calmed down, although every so often, a flashback will come into my head *That's So Raven*-style that stops me in my tracks and

I'm right in that moment again like I've been transported back to war.

While I know there's every chance I'll eventually be able to live something close to a normal life again, I also know that none of this will ever leave me because it is now part of my psychological makeup. I still cringe about things I did eight years ago and they penetrate my mind when I'm least expecting it, which is why I can't ever do ayahuasca, because then everything will come to the fore and I don't have the mental capacity to handle that.

⚢

You can't stop hangxiety. I don't care how supportive your friends are or how much they're willing to lie to you about your behaviour the night before to make it sound less abysmal, it is coming for you. Unless, that is, you're someone who genuinely doesn't give a shit about anything – like Ella, for example, and this is the major difference between us.

A perfect illustration of that came in the early weeks of us dating in 2024. She was off-season and had gone to a bottomless brunch with two of her friends and must have been a few bottles deep when she text asking me to come and join them. We ended up heading to a club in Mayfair where it costs something vile like two grand for the table plus a massive bottle of Grey Goose.

We'd only had about five drinks from it when we decided we'd had enough of this place and were ready to leave, but the club rules stated that taking the vodka with us wasn't allowed. You use it or lose it.

'Guys,' I said, 'I haven't paid all this money for a bottle of vodka to not then take it home.'

So we swipe it and run towards the doors, chased by the security until Ella puts the bottle down her trousers and says to the bouncers, 'If you put your hands in there to get it, I will report you.'

OK, wow.

They had no other option but to let us run off into the night but the next day, my hangxiety was through the roof. Why?

1. Because I was worried that Ella's friends who I'd only just met would think I was a dick, and:
2. I was *petrified* someone had filmed us shouting at the security and we were about to go viral on social media.

But while I was emotionally and mentally crashing out, Ella was just delighted with herself, happily getting on with her day. We're just built differently.

We can never return to that club, obviously. And when I say that, I mean not within a mile of the place ever again.

Hangover cures that definitely maybe work

- Timing your departure. Nothing good happens after 1am. I'm a firm believer in Irish exits. Like, why am I hugging 16 people and prolonging my own agony? Just no.
- Full faceplant in a bowl of cold water.
- Brush your teeth as quickly as possible.
- Shower at the earliest opportunity to wash away the sins of the previous night.
- Approximately a gallon of Orange Lucozade.
- Paracetamol.
- Anti-sickness tablets.
- Make sure you expel that post-alcohol shit before you leave the house. A truly spiritual experience.
- If at work, fake it. Do not even mention that you feel hungover; you can die when you get home later.
- Start drinking again. Sometimes it's the only way, guys.

The worst place in the world to wake up with a hangover? Anywhere that's not your own house. When that happens, on top of the complete mental breakdown you're already dealing with, you now also have to travel home wearing the clothes you had on last night. Horrific.

Basically, if you're getting drunk, you'd best come home by any means possible that night because travelling while hungover is a disgusting decision. I've had to take a two-hour train ride hanging out my arse, during which my soul left my body and I'm not sure it's ever returned.

I've also been forced to do a plane journey back from Ibiza on a hangover so violent I thought I was having a stroke. And I know this is not relatable whatsoever because it happened to be on a private jet but, believe me, that was arguably worse because it felt like I was being rocketed to the moon.

One small mercy is that I'm rarely physically sick with it. I have emetophobia – a fear of vomit – after a boy called Morgan Ward hurled up all over the table in Year 5, and when I've had that to contend with on top of the hangxiety, it just about puts me in rehab. Like the time a couple of years back when I'd been to an event where they were serving a free bar of spiced rum and Coke. Now, I'd never had spiced rum before and, my God, it tasted sensational. I didn't even feel that drunk, but I do remember I suddenly felt the need to leave. So I pulled my usual vanishing act and headed home, smug that I'd got out in the nick of time.

POV: the next morning.

I wake up and I'm lying on the sofa. My heating has broken and it's the middle of winter, so I'm physically shaking from what I conclude is terminal pneumonia. I have no food in the house because I've not long moved in and haven't done a big shop. Or any kind of shop.

I run into the downstairs bathroom and lie on the floor so I'm now curled up in the foetal position in the coldest place in the house, possibly even on Earth itself, but I'm still overheating.

That's when I start throwing up. I'm wearing an Oodie and am trying to take it off over my head while vomiting, which is not a task for the weak. And I am so very weak.

For a few minutes post-sickness, I feel semi-human again and kid myself that the ordeal is over. I can now take the day to rest and fully recover. All is well.

I walk gingerly back to the sofa with a vague plan to watch all that daytime TV has to offer, but no sooner have I settled down, the nausea returns and I have to crawl back to the bathroom for round two.

This is it. This is how I'm going to die.

There's nothing else for it. I call my mum, hysterically crying.

'I need you.'

'What do you expect us to do, Grace?'

'I'm so unwell. I neeeeed you.'

My liver was in physical pain at this point. All I wanted was to be in a house with my parents where they could make me cups of tea, feed me paracetamol, tuck me into a blanket, plump up my pillows and basically do everything for me. By the afternoon, I made a snap decision, got in my car and did the two-hour drive back to the village, retching for the whole journey, desperately trying to keep my shit together until I got to my mum and dad's where, upon arrival, I promptly threw up again.

It was next-level alcohol poisoning and I bravely cheated death for the next two and a half days. That was the Wednesday and I swore blind I was never drinking again.

Guys, I drank again on the Friday.

All of this gets inevitably worse with age. When I had a proper job, I could get in at 2am, wake up at five and open the Costa I worked at while still pissed. Yep, I might start to flag a bit halfway through my shift and I'd have even less patience with the general public than usual, but I'd still be able to go out and do it all again that night. I was a warrior back then. As soon as the clock strikes 12 on your 21st birthday ... strap in, queens.

⚢

If I have to go to work now with a hangover, heaven help me: I've got cold compresses, Imodium, anti-sickness pills and Lucozades coming out my arse and they aren't even registering.

The most catastrophic hangover experience I've ever had at work came in February 2023. I'm sharing this now to unburden myself as well as to provide you all with a warning, so consider this a PSA. I'd been out celebrating the final date of my second podcast tour in The Box in London's Soho. The drinks were flowing and I was loving life in there until I got outside, saw it was daylight and thought, 'Oh sweet baby Jesus, no.'

The clock on my phone told me it was 6am. Six. In normal circumstances this wouldn't be a major problem, but your girl is hosting the BRITs red carpet that day and has to be at her management's offices for glam for nine.

And so began the worst day of my entire life.

It was 7.30am by the time I arrived home, where I put my head on the pillow for what felt like a minute before waking up to the sound of my alarm (thank fuck I'd remembered to set it) ringing like the chimes of doom at half past eight.

There's a car waiting outside the house for me, ready to take me back to London where there are people expecting me to be able to string whole sentences together. I somehow make it out of bed and into said car and I'm driven to my management HQ where I'm now in the pits of hell. It's fight or flight. Someone somewhere produces a bottle of Prosecco. I realise I have to carry on drinking and the rest is history.

It will come as no surprise to you to learn that I was shit at all those red-carpet interviews. I spoke to Dua Lipa and said to her, 'Who am I here with?'

'What are you talking about?' she replied, laughing. 'Do you not know who I am?'

And, to be fair, I didn't at the time because I was pissed. You could have put Kim Kardashian in front of me and my mind would have been completely blank. I will be thinking about this at 3am forever.

Things I've done drunk that have made me consider changing my identity

- Squared up to people in nightclubs even though I couldn't fight my way out of a paper bag and would probably get swept away by a gust of wind. That was when I knew I had to knock the bottomless brunches on the head.
- Vomited in a boyfriend's bin the first night I stayed over at his and then his mum came in to collect and dispose of it. Shameful. From that day forward I have never touched peach schnapps.
- Revealed people's secrets. I bumped into a hen do once and the girls told me there was a stripper coming as a surprise for the bride but not to say anything. It must have been a whole two minutes before I said to the bride, 'When's the stripper arriving?'
- Slagged people off to people who know them, which then means they'll confront me with this information and force me into lying through my teeth. 'Did they say I said that? That's so weird. I think you need to check with them because I definitely didn't say that.'
- Taken a piss in public everywhere imaginable.
- Approached the comedian Josh Widdicombe and said, 'Gobble, gobble,' which is the code word for listeners

to his *Parenting Hell* podcast with Rob Beckett. 'Ah,' said Josh, 'you like the pod?' 'Yeah,' I replied, 'I don't even have kids. I actually hate kids, but I might get a surrogate and have a baby just so I can come on as a guest.' Josh looked at me with a mix of fear and pity before walking off.

- Theft. Glasses from pubs, other people's vapes (probably contracting hepatitis C in the process), traffic cones. At uni I'd wake up with so many traffic cones from the night before it looked like the M25 in my room.

- One night I couldn't afford a taxi home, so I nicked an unattended bike from Newmarket High Street and then posted on Snapchat, 'Lol, just stole a bike.' It only went viral, didn't it? Turned out it was a child's bike so I obviously returned it, but I nearly got fired from my job at Costa because of that.

- At my 21st birthday, I had a party in my parents' garden. I was wearing a top that had slipped up, meaning both my tits were out and on display as I took to the floor to sing 'WAP' directly at my mother. I don't even swear in front of my parents normally and so to be singing about Wet Ass Pussy was quite the leap. She kicked everyone out shortly afterwards. And then I cried.

There are so many things I've done and said while drunk that I've tried to block out to protect my mental wellbeing, but every one of my most appalling mistakes has been made after pre-drinking with Echo Falls wine.

I have no filter after two Proseccos and once I've had a tequila or a sambuca, I'm blacked out. I don't remember what happens until some well-meaning person-slash-psychopath with a photographic memory informs me the next day, but I am learning what those drinks do to me. Now, if someone offers me a tequila shot, I will tell them to go fuck themselves because if I accept it, I know I will wake up in a random house with no idea how I got there.

My mum, on the other hand, can drink four bottles of wine and not only will she avoid a hangover but she'll also remember everything that's occurred. So that extra-special 'WAP' performance is stored permanently in her memory bank.

My biggest problem with alcohol is that when I'm drunk, I don't think I'm drunk. In my head, I'm 100 per cent sober, not a drop in my system. The room might well be spinning, but as far as I'm concerned, that last drink hasn't touched the sides. In fact, I'm so definitely not drunk that I think someone must have given me something non-alcoholic by mistake, so please get me another and make it a double.

I don't know where the line is, and even if I get home at a sensible time, I'll get into bed and carry on drinking there, often while scrolling through GoFundMe and donating like

I'm Mother Teresa. When I see a kid I don't know who needs a new wheelchair or someone whose mum's just died, it hits me right in the heart.

How much have they got left to fundraise? I'll cover it. Some mornings I wake up and realise that on top of spending hundreds of pounds buying randomers drinks, I've also saved Carol from Portsmouth from a brain tumour.

If you ever need help for a worthy cause, send me a crowdfunder link at about 9pm on a Friday, because you will be getting a donation.

Alcohol: cause and effect

- **White wine**: Ready to gossip and tell you the life story of everyone I know all night.
- **Red wine**: Don't know what it is, but red has a violence ingredient for me and I'm probably going to end up in jail on it one day.
- **Prosecco**: Similar vibes to white wine, but I will fall asleep mid-conversation with you after two hours.
- **Sambuca**: The devil's juice. If I so much as smell it, I will be in a coffin.
- **Tequila**: Makes me the happiest drunk and keeps me going till the early hours, but the hangover is not worth it.

- **Schnapps**: Can't touch it. It reminds me of being 14 and it tastes like tar.
- **Vodka**: Dangerous because I don't realise I'm drunk and think I'm being sensible as well as hilarious until the next day when I don't remember anything and I become very concerned about where my life choices have led me.
- **Cactus Jack's**: Horror and hell.
- **BuzzBallz**: Beautiful, delicious, could climb Kilimanjaro after downing six and also feel like a proper Suffragette because it's a female-founded company.

Alcohol gives me confidence and I think I become funnier when I'm drunk, hence I used to do TV shows while pissed as a fart.* There have been times on the late-night shows where I've been close to blackout and, after rambling on, chatting shit, it gives me hangxiety for days.

I can't even argue with the people in the comments.

'She doesn't know what she's talking about. Why have you got her on?'

And I'm like, 'You're absolutely right, Sandra.'

Some TV shows actively encourage it. *Love Island: Aftersun* gave me a bottle of champagne in my room before we went on air, FFS, so what's a girl to do?

---

* Not *Loose Women*, I hasten to add, although maybe I should try it.

If you're teetotal, I think good for you. I'm sure it's incredible to go through life without ever waking up and wanting to book yourself in for a lobotomy. But the truth is, I'd struggle to do a night out without alcohol. I don't like dancing and so going to a club sober, for me, is a hate crime and anyway, some of the best times in my life have happened when drunk – they've been all the better because everyone was wasted.

Even during Covid, when we were only allowed to see three or four people, me and my three friends would go drinking in a field and we laughed the whole time. I lost my glasses on one of those piss-ups and couldn't see for about three months because there were no appointments available at Specsavers.

Until the bad times outweigh the good and it's time to check into The Priory, I suppose I'll be here flatlining, freaking out and reflecting on the many mistakes from the night before.

I've accepted my fate at this point.

CHAPTER FIVE

Dating Dramas

Icks, virginity, worst dates and relationship red flags

If my dating profile was truthful ...

'Obscenely lazy. Flat arse, no tits, posture resembles a shrimp. Will give minus ten for effort in the bedroom. Lights on, top on – that's my motto; if you don't like it, we can have no future together. Promise to be the funniest person you'll ever be with and willing to cook you food, but do not look at my Instagram because all pictures are edited and my life is a sham.'

⚢

The first male who made me sit up and think, *Hang on a minute, this is a bit of me*, was Justin Bieber. I loved that boy with his beautiful face, baby-bottom skin and fringe sweep, and I had posters of him plastered all over my bedroom walls. I have no idea why we all wet our knickers for that look, but I guess that was the 2010s which was generally a more wholesome time.

Other crushes included Jedward (still love me a bit of John and Edward), the mentally unstable energy of the emo guy from Bring Me the Horizon and that *X Factor* boy Frankie Cocozza after I was completely taken in by the hellraising bad-boy act. Remember how we were all treating him like one of the Sex Pistols when actually he was some no-mark from Brighton on a reality-TV talent show your nan voted on?

This was long before I caught the bus to the Land of Lez and back then it was only boys I was into. At school I had two guys I flipped between, each for a few months at a time. One was tall and scrawny, and the other was stumpy and more muscular. So, quite clearly, I didn't have a type.

How you'd start seeing someone on MSN*

'Hey u ok?'

'Yeh.'

'Me 2.'

'Wot u up 2 x'

(That kiss sign-off was the critical turning point, putting the ball in their court.)

'Nothing much x'

(A kiss back. You're in.)

How you'd get dumped on MSN

'Wots wrong'

'I don't think we can be together rn'

'Cool'

* Imagine WhatsApp but cooler.

I had my first kiss in my bedroom while my mum and dad were downstairs watching *A Place in the Sun*. I'd been so scared beforehand despite extensive preparation work, which involved practising on the mirror, my hand and on an old doll who was, upon reflection, terribly abused.

In desperation, I'd googled important things like 'how long do you put your tongue in for?' and 'will my braces get in the way?' but when it finally happened, I realised it was completely overhyped. Funnily enough, during that same encounter I also gave my first blow job because I thought, *In for a penny, in for a pound*, and that while we were at it, I might as well get that out the way, too. It proved to be a reckless decision on my part which provoked an immediate stress response, thinking that I could now be pregnant.

I turned to Google again and asked whether it was possible to be impregnated from a blow job and, let me tell you, the answer I was given was not reassuring. The internet showed me no mercy that day and basically told me that if any semen (urgh) had gone within two metres of the fanny then there was a chance I could be with child.

And so now my cortisol levels are spiking and I'm spiralling, kicking myself for not waiting until I was 16 because 'pregnant at 16' somehow doesn't seem half as bad as 'pregnant at 15'.

For the record, you can't get pregnant from a blow job.

I'm not sure if my parents knew I was doing bits with boys (one time I got sperm in my eye which made it go all bloodshot and I had to pass it off as conjunctivitis), but if I'd tried to talk to my mum about shagging or anything like that, there's no way she'd have made it to the age she is now and neither would my dad.

Neither of them were ever particularly warm to any boyfriend I introduced them to. In fact, my dad actively hated them all and it's only Ella that they've managed to bother their arses to be nice to. With one guy I was dating, my dad came out to greet him literally armed with an axe. He meant it as a joke, but I died a thousand deaths and had to apologise on his behalf.

'I'm sorry, my dad has the same warped sense of humour as I do. It's a Caribbean thing.'

Virginity: the naked facts*

- Median age for the first time in the UK is 17. This means half of people have had sex by around this age.
- Around 19 per cent of Brits said they had sex before they turned 16, the legal age of consent in the UK.
- Girls are more likely to have had sex by the age of 16 than boys (40 per cent versus 31 per cent).

* Stats from YouGov 2023.

I know that as a girl your virginity often feels like being caught between a rock and a hard place. Pun intended. Because boys are horrible little creatures who can't keep their mouths shut, where I was from, you either did it and had everyone know about it or it was put about everyone that you were 'frigid'.

On the day I lost mine, my mum had popped out to Sainsbury's and I said to my boyfriend at the time, 'Let's just get this over and done with.' I'd heard all the horror stories about how you bleed and basically die, so I was keen to get it done as quickly as possible.

And indeed, it was done quickly. Very quickly. I'm not even sure it was in, if I'm honest.

I'd seen sex scenes in films where the whole process looked absolutely mental, but this by comparison was, for want of a better word, shit.

I think getting a root canal done would have been more joyous.

And then he went into school on the Monday, told everyone we'd done it and that I'd laid there like a dead fish. Like I said, horrible little creatures. One of the bitchiest popular girls then posted that picture of a dead fish on Twitter I mentioned earlier, so that was me scarred for life.

The thing is, virginity is built up to be this big deal. But you don't actually 'lose' anything when you have sex for the first time and, hand on heart, I don't think it's half as important as some people make it out to be. I never give it a second thought now or wish that I'd waited longer and I doubt when I'm 50, I'm going to be sitting there punching walls about it.

I wasn't ever like, 'This is such a sacred moment.'

Having said that, I definitely *did* think it was a vital part of being in a relationship. This was just what you did and I thought I'd get dumped if I didn't go along with it.

'If I don't do this, he'll just go with someone who will' is a fucked-up reason to have sex with anyone, but it was only years later that I learned sleeping with someone doesn't mean they'll like you more. Or that they'll stay with you over someone else. Real connection doesn't work like that and feelings don't become stronger just because something physical happened.

Relationship red flags

- Being made to feel you need to change who you are – never let anyone do that.
- If they've recently split up with someone then I'm afraid you're the rebound and you need to get the hell out.
- Straight men who have a lot of female 'friends'. Like, nope. We all know they just want to fuck them.
- People who are friends with exes. This is actually really common on the lesbian scene and I am not down for it. I think it's weird and should be illegal.
- If they don't like dogs. Get out of town.

I've honestly never been on a proper first date in my life. I used to love a bit of Hinge purely for the emotional reassurance it gave me to know that someone somewhere thought I was fit. But I've never actually gone to meet up with anyone from a dating app mainly because I've watched too much true crime.

Even apart from the risk of being turned into a Netflix documentary, I simply can't deal with the cringe of a first date – getting stuck with a stranger having a meal together is a scary amount of commitment too early on. And the thought of doing an activity – bowling, mini golf, ice skating or anything that involves me having to do something while being watched – makes me feel very unwell.

The closest I've come to a first date was with a drug dealer who had half a front tooth and lived in a hostel. He asked me out and then made me drive to McDonald's where I managed to leave the car headlights on, meaning my battery died while we were inside fine dining on Big Macs and chicken nuggets which, I believe, I paid for. We then had to jumpstart the car which, as you can probably imagine, was great fun and then we went back to the hostel where I slept with him.

If you've had a bleaker first date, let me know.

I did get quite into him though and when my parents said there was no way he was spending Christmas with us, I was livid.

'Well then, I'm going to spend Christmas at the hostel,' I said.

I should not have done that. Christmas Day in a hostel was a humbling experience, and the whole time I questioned why I was there when I literally had a home.

But I was too stubborn to back down.

Hostel boy was just one of a series of inappropriate, unsuitable or generally dickish specimens I've been out with. There was a guy from college I'd been seeing for about a year when he went off to Reading Festival for five days. I didn't go, due to the fact I wasn't invited and also because I would rather die than go to a festival. Grass, mud, people throwing up everywhere and having to sleep in a tent – that is my version of Death Row.

Anyway, he gets back from Reading and I notice that he's retweeted one of his best friends saying how amazing the weekend had been. And a girl who I don't know has liked his retweet.

What the fuck?

I click on her profile and, oh 'ello. Why is her Twitter cover photo a picture of my boyfriend and her cuddling?

I send him a screenshot of her profile and got straight to the point.

'Who the fuck is this?'

I was fuming, foaming at the mouth, and he was crying, swearing on his life that nothing happened. But it was too late. I knew he was lying so I broke up with him and thankfully the timing was sweet because it was the end of the college year and so I didn't ever have to see him again.

It was savage at the time and let me be clear that cheating is shit, but I don't bear any hard feelings because I think it's pretty normal when you're young and in a relationship. This isn't the 1900s; we don't get betrothed to the person we're seeing at 15. When you meet a better option, yes, you should probably dump your boyfriend or girlfriend first, but we famously don't have backbones at that age. So you do what you gotta do.

⚢

There was another charmer of an ex who tried to run me over in his car. I'd just started uni in Nottingham and had been dating this guy back home out of pure boredom. He was really rough, had a baby who I knew he never saw and he'd also been to prison on 21 assault charges.

Quite the catch.

After my first week at uni, it was like my brain unlocked and I realised I was done with him, so I text to say it was over then switched off my phone, went on a night out and thought no more about it.

When I turned the phone back on, it blew up. There were messages, voicemails and a voice note from a mutual friend warning me this guy was on his way up to have it out with me. I assumed they were taking the piss. After all, this was at 3am and he lived in Cambridge which was 90 miles away. But, as I arrive back to my halls of residence, pissed as a fart and with two male flatmates, he's parked outside. And, on top of everything else, he now thinks I'm heading back for a threesome which sends him into a rage.

He puts his foot on the gas and drives straight at me. My flatmates completely abandon me, running into the halls. Thankfully, I manage to reach the main door of the building which I access with my fob and then slam shut behind me.

So now he's on the outside of this locked glass door shouting to be let in when this student girl who I've never even seen before arrives from upstairs wanting to get out.

'Don't open the door,' I tell her. 'You can't let him in.'

This bitch clearly has places to be, so she opens the door and lets him in.

Me and my flatmates are now running through the halls to get away from him and he's going crazy but eventually runs out of steam and is escorted out by security while shouting that he's going to kill himself. He then sends me a dramatic message saying, 'By the time you get this, I will be dead.'

Fuck my life.

Because of that, I had no choice but to phone the police, who came to the halls and then called his mum to check on his welfare.

'Oh, he always does this,' she said, totally unconcerned. 'He's perfectly fine, he's sitting in the living room.'

Well. The second-hand shame I felt. I thought, *That is so embarrassing for you*, and I never spoke to him again after that.

Heartbreak cures that definitely work

- Listening to Megan Thee Stallion or, if you're really down, Lewis Capaldi, but it's crucial that you snap the hell out of this phase extremely quickly.
- Focusing on the post-relationship rebrand – you've got time to work on looking as hot as possible now in order to start posting the revenge thirst traps on socials.
- Go to Ibiza. Specifically, Ocean Beach, where you too can have your picture taken hanging out with Wayne Lineker and all will be well.
- Regular rants to your best friend until they eventually tell you to STFU and you know it's time to move on.
- Hyper-fixating on a new hobby. Drugs, for instance. I'm joking, I'm joking. Pilates would be more appropriate in this situation.
- Bottomless brunches with the girlies.
- Blocking your ex but maintaining a fake profile so you can still watch their every move. Do not be caught in the act with your actual government name. During one deep dive on an ex, I accidentally liked a photo from several years before and didn't realise until he messaged a mutual friend to ask, 'Why the fuck has Grace just liked a picture from three years ago?' A rookie error.

- Wine. Sometimes only alcohol will do.

More often than not, it's me who's done the dumping at the end of a relationship. However, I fully admit that I've not always dealt with it as sensitively as I could have. I broke up with one boyfriend while I was secretly filming the whole thing to show my friend how it all went. We were walking out of school and I turned to him and said, 'I don't really want to be with you anymore.'

He kind of gulped and there was an awkward pause.

'OK,' he replied, his voice catching, 'like, can we hug?'

So I said 'all right' and then I sent the clip to my mate who sent it to another mate, who sent it to everyone else and so within the space of 20 minutes, the whole school had seen me break up with him.

I know, I'm an arsehole.

When he pulled me up on it, I went full gaslighter and said I hadn't realised I was recording and didn't even know how the video had got out.

The one time I was left completely heartbroken by the end of a relationship was when the hostel boy dumped me after a year together and it honestly felt like having my insides ripped out. What made it worse was that he got a new girlfriend straight afterwards and I spent the next six months avidly stalking both their Instagrams and Facebooks while using fake accounts with names like @SkintSpice.

I'd do regular drive-bys at the hostel to see if I could catch them together, trying to keep tabs on whether she was round there, and although I probably should have been served with an injunction, that was my way of coping.

And then came the sucker punch.

There was a pub in Ely where everyone would go and one of his friends approached me in there and said that while we'd been together, he'd been cheating on me with a girl I knew. And, well, after a few Jägerbombs, I picked up the phone and left him a message. 'You're a prick, I hate you and I hope you don't wake up from your nap!'

He messaged me back to say I was actually psychopathic and we've never spoken since.

Single life

Pros

- Freedom.
- Not having anyone to depend on or answer to.
- Zero drama.
- Getting your mental bandwidth back.
- The glow-up from being forced into getting hot in order to spite the ex.

Cons

- Chronic loneliness. It's giving 2020.
- The hell of coming home to an empty house.
- Late-night existential thoughts.
- No Christmas or birthday gifts. What is the point of even being alive?

When I'm single, I will throw myself into work. I become a rabid wild animal, which isn't sustainable and eventually I will break. Just before I moved into the first house I'd bought myself, I told my then-boyfriend I didn't want to be with him anymore. That relationship had definitely run its course, but the downside of suddenly being single was that I was now rattling around this three-bedroom semi on my own in an area where I didn't know anyone. I had no dogs for company at that time and so my evenings would just be me sitting in front of the telly or cleaning in order to stave off a mental health episode. I would deep clean the house, putting my cloths to bed in the sink every night like Mrs Hinch, who, by the way, I love. She's my go-to my comfort creator.

To fill the gap, and because I can't be alone, I worked an insane amount every day, even weekends, doing 12-hour shoots and saying yes to anything that came in, just to save myself from my own company.

I was earning great money, but it got to the point where I was all worked out and wanted something more. I'm much less impulsive in a relationship because I have someone there to rein me in and say, 'Grace, this is probably not a great idea for you.'

If you're single and don't want to be, try not to put any pressure on yourself to find The One. The chances are, you're going to spend most of your life in a relationship further down the line, so while you still have the chance, enjoy doing all the things you should be doing as a single person. And those things are, unquestionably, going out, getting paralytic, snogging randoms and vomiting in taxis.

The GK Barry ick list

- Seeing them walking down a hill. That leaning back and awkward run-slash-limp makes me feel physically ill. No walking down a hill until we're at least six months in, please, otherwise there is no point in us continuing.
- Specifically for men, having a mum who is obsessed with their son. That is so fucking weird and I don't like it.
- Bad manners, especially in restaurants if they're not nice to waiters or waitresses.
- Having no goals in life; I find that so gross.

- Being a drug dealer. No further explanation required.
- First-date burping or farting; a hard pass from me.
- Skinny jeans. Nope.
- Boys who wear loafers with no socks.

My relationships usually have an expiry date of one year. By the time I've done a straight 365 days, I'm either so bored that I want to die, they've pissed me off beyond the point of forgiveness or I have the ick so bad that I feel personally attacked by their mere presence.

The last guy I was with before I turned lesbian told me he wanted to start doing social media and that was it for me. Like, no. You're in recruitment and now you've just given me the ick of all icks and this has to end.

Ella is the only one to make it past the year mark. She's never boring, only annoys me very occasionally and doesn't ever give me the ick. She could literally sit there and bite her toenails off and I'd be like, 'Oh my God, that's so lovely. I love you!'

So I guess she's a keeper.

Before we move on ...

TRIGGER WARNING

This part contains content related to sexual violence

OK, guys, this is going to be a bit of a gear change. Up until now I've been sharing some of the most ridiculous stories from my life but this next one isn't quite like that. I'm about to tell you something that happened to me when I was 17, which I've carried ever since, and I'm not going to try and make light of it because that wouldn't be right or honest of me.

I've actually thought about whether to share it at all, but if speaking out helps even a handful of you reading this, then it's been worth it.

Just stay with me.

In my second year of college, I managed to get a week's work experience at a media company. It wasn't close to where we lived and on my second day there, I couldn't get a lift from my mum, so the guy I was reporting to offered to pick me up on his way in.

He was about 27 so around ten years older, attractive, tattooed and muscly, and I was impressed by him – we'd been having a bit of text back and forth and, admittedly, I was flattered that he was giving me the time of day. However, as we were driving in that morning, he kept touching my leg which was making me feel uncomfortable although I didn't feel able to ask him to stop. There was a massive imbalance of power going on which he was 100 per cent taking advantage of, banking on the fact I wouldn't push back.

He asked me where I wanted to go and I said to the office, obviously. But he said he was taking me to the park instead.

I knew this was all kinds of wrong, my instinct was screaming that I was in trouble here and I prayed that there would be other people in the park. I told myself nothing bad could happen if there were other people around.

But when we got there, it was deserted.

He walked me down to some trees and said, 'Right, to be blunt, suck me off.'

'What?'

'Suck me off,' he said again.

And so I did. I didn't know what else I could do except go along with what he was telling me – resisting or fighting back felt like it might make things worse. There was never a moment in my mind where I thought I could say no to what was happening because a) I had no way of getting home and b) I was doing work experience with him which I needed to pass my course. When you're 17 and scared as fuck, thinking logically isn't an option.

Once it was over, he took me into work where we had a normal day and he carried on as if nothing had happened for the rest of the week.

At 4pm on my last day, he kicked out the two other members of staff who were there, leaving only me and him in the building.

I start to panic because I feel like I know what's about to happen but I'm powerless to stop it. He signals me towards a side room, making a point of saying there are no cameras in there and I go in because, again, there's no ability in my body to refuse. I'm also pretty certain he's locked the office, so I'm trapped.

He closes the door behind us and tells me to take my trousers off. I do as I'm told and remove my white jeans.

And then he rapes me.

It's taken me a long time – years, in fact – to realise that's what it was. Even longer to be able to say it out loud. I blamed myself. I hadn't said no, so wasn't it basically consensual? Maybe I'd led him on – I'd definitely flirted with him before that car journey. I also had a boyfriend at the time and worried that this meant I'd cheated on him.

Straight afterwards he said, 'OK you can go home now.' I was in shock, in pain and bleeding, and as I put my white jeans back on, I remember thinking, *Thank God I have a long coat with me to cover up the blood.*

I changed as soon as I got home and when my mum asked what the hell had happened to my trousers, I told her I'd just come on my period.

I didn't tell a soul, not even my closest friends. I even asked my boyfriend if he would class it as cheating if someone had forced themselves on me and his response was, 'Well, it depends what you'd done to give them that idea.' So that just cemented in my brain that this was my fault.

For almost a whole year I stayed silent. In the meantime, this guy would come into Costa where I worked and my stomach dropped every time. I'd start shaking and nothing in my mind would compute – he'd be ordering a coffee but I couldn't even put it through the till. The only other time I've had a similar physical reaction is when I was about to do a bungee jump.

It wasn't until one of my teachers at college told me that another girl from the course was going to do work experience at the same place where I knew this guy still worked that I told anyone. I knew I couldn't let her go, so I asked for a quiet word with the teacher and told her that something had happened to me during work experience that shouldn't have. I didn't use the word 'rape', but my teacher immediately caught on that this was serious.

She called a female colleague in and they said we had to tell the police as well as my mum, to which I thought, *OK, so now I have to die.* I'm very open with my mum now, but at the time I would never have dreamed of talking to her about anything like that.

Anyway, they call her in, so now I'm in the canteen of Cambridge Reject College telling my mother what he did and it sends her into full spiral, upset that she hadn't been able to protect me from it and freaking out about how she's going to stop my dad going off and killing the bloke.

A few days later, a female police officer came into college and showed me to her unmarked car outside where she said we could talk in private. This was where she told me that, in her opinion, there was very little point in taking this further because I hadn't reported it at the time and I'd described some mild flirting between me and him beforehand. All of which, she said, would look bad in court.

There had also been contact between us afterwards because the guy had messaged me on and off since it happened and I'd replied as if we were mates. Fuck, I'd even served him in Costa.

At no point did the police officer say to me that what he'd done was wrong.

And then it was just left. There wasn't any support offered to me at the college or even a suggestion that I might want to speak to someone about it. I'm not actually sure if I'd have done that, but it would have been nice to know someone was there if I needed.

I wish I'd known that it wasn't my fault. I wish I'd known what to be on guard for. I'd had no idea that rape can take so many different forms and it doesn't always look the way you expect. I think we imagine it to be a stranger attack in a dark alley, but it's far more likely to happen between people who know each other – friends, partners, classmates or colleagues. It can involve pressure and manipulation or someone like me who does not give consent but falls into line out of fear or a weird power dynamic.

When I think of a nonce or paedo or any man who takes advantage of young girls, I think of a 60-year-old perv who looks like Jimmy Savile. But really, any older man showing an interest in a younger girl should send alarm bells ringing. When I was at school, some of the girls in my year were talking to guys who were in their twenties and we never had anyone explaining to us that this was actually really weird and inappropriate. It's not normal for a grown man to want a relationship with a teenager.

All this has been a huge eye-opener into how men can operate and abuse their positions and there are some really important conversations to be had so that girls are better informed and prepared for what the realities are in the wider world. They need to know where to get help if they find themselves in a situation like mine and I would love the opportunity to go into schools and talk to girls – and boys as well – about this.

And I know it's not all men, but it's *always* men and it's *every* woman and girl. All of us will have had an experience of predatory behaviour on some level, whether it's being randomly groped or letched on, all the way up to the most serious offence.

I was lucky that I had a great friendship group and a good home life but I can still count on one hand the number of people I've felt able to tell. I've never even spoken about it to my mum since – the first time it's been mentioned again was when I told her I was going to be writing about it in this book and she gave me her blessing.

Those who do know have reassured me that I didn't do anything wrong and sharing has helped, but one of the reasons I've been frightened to talk about it is in case someone confirms my biggest fear that I was to blame.

I also carry quite a bit of guilt. Because he was so confident about what he did, I'm sure I wasn't the first and won't have been the last, and maybe I could have stopped him from doing this to another girl. But although I wish now I'd reported it at the time, I also feel really strongly that it's not women's fucking responsibility to stop men raping us.

It's made me a lot more wary and I still don't really enjoy working with older men, which is why I love that my management team are all female. But I don't think about it half as much as I used to. Sometimes I get a trigger and can't help but search his name on the internet to see if I can find him and what he's doing, but not so often these days.

I do still dread the possibility of bumping into him though, because I feel sure he would think it was fine to stop and say hello. And I'd probably have a conversation with him because I'd do anything not to make a situation uncomfortable.

Mad, isn't it?

If reading this has brought up some difficult feelings or affected you in any way, know that there is help out there. If it feels wrong, it is wrong. No one has the right to make you feel pressured, unsafe or trapped, and if you find yourself in a situation like this:

- Reach out to someone you trust.
- Speak to the practice nurse at your local GP surgery.
- Call the support line run by Rape Crisis which is open 24/7 on 0808 500 2222.
- Or use their online chat at rapecrisis.org.uk

It's taken me the best part of ten years to realise it was a big deal and it did matter.

You are not alone.

CHAPTER SIX

University Challenge

Drugs, drink and dicking about

For pretty much the entire four years I was at uni, I was incredibly stoned. To this day I have literally no idea how I emerged with anything resembling a degree because whenever I had an assignment of any kind to do, someone would suggest getting high instead and I'd end up doing the square root of fuck all.

My student loan and overdraft were spent on weed, Pot Noodles, Echo Falls wine, discounted £1 cakes from the corner shop.

But mostly weed.

I would have chosen that over a meal any day of the week and access to it was made even easier when, halfway through the first year, a new guy (who I'll call Trevor) moved into our student halls flat. Trevor, so it turned out, was a massive drug dealer. He had two kids with two different women, neither of whom he saw, and he was also the city of Nottingham's chief pimp. Trevor was a busy boy.

There would be random people coming to our flat at all hours – friends or customers of Trev's, who knows? – and none of us knew why he was in the halls of residence because he was about 35 and certainly never went to uni or appeared to do any form of studying. I'm also unsure as to where the duty of care was from the people running Nottingham Trent's accommodation services in placing him with us. He was nice enough, but there was always the distinct feeling that he could blow at any minute and, indeed, he's in jail now. I know this because I recently got him on Snapchat.

'Free Trevor!' I messaged him. 'Hope you're OK.'

'What the fuck has happened to you?' he replied from what I presume was his burner phone. 'I've literally just seen you on the telly.'

'Yeah … maybe keep how we know each other to yourself.'

Anyway, to cut a long story short, Trevor became our supplier and it was downhill from there, like a diabetic being forced to work in a cake factory.

Just say no, kids.

Pie chart of my average uni week

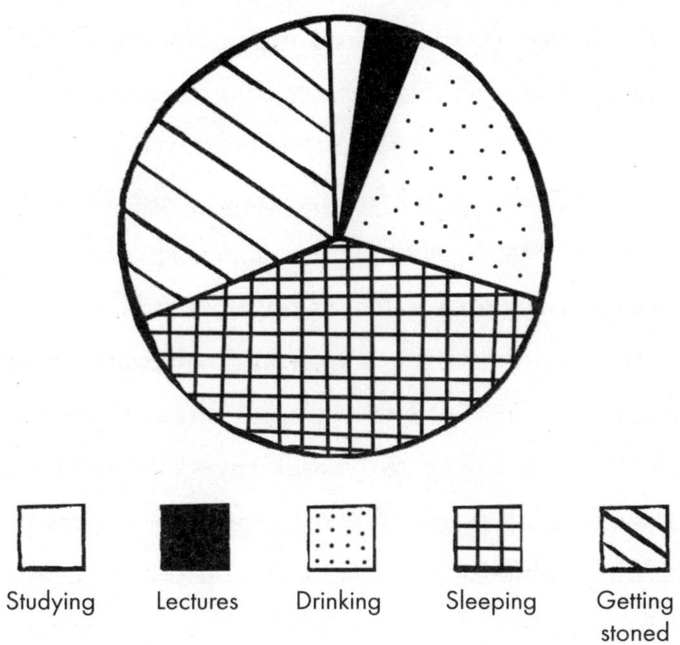

Going to university hadn't exactly been top of my to-do list. During my three years at college, I didn't really know where my life was heading or what I wanted to do with the rest of it, but in the end I had my mind made up for me by my dad. He sat me down and told me I had to hit the high road because he wasn't allowing me to stay in the village.

'You're going to university,' he said. 'I don't care which uni it is but that's what you're doing because you need to leave this town before you end up pregnant.'

Bit harsh.

At the time, I'd more or less moved into the hostel with my drug-dealing boyfriend which I thought was the coolest thing ever but, as you can probably appreciate, my parents weren't feeling it. I don't actually think I *would* have fallen pregnant because I despise small children with every fibre of my soul so I'd have been careful not to let that happen. But I accept now that for many other reasons, if I'd stayed where I was, it wouldn't have been good for me. I'd become so chronically anxious that I spent most of my time holed up at the hostel and I wasn't able to get on a train or a bus by myself.

All this mainly stemmed from my emetophobia and the fact that every time I left the house, I was struck with panic that either I was going to be sick myself or someone was going to throw up near me. If it happened on a bus or train, I wouldn't be able to get off quickly and the thought of that left me in a mess.

It was only when I was *forced* to do those things by moving away and living on my own that I started to overcome my fears, because at uni if I didn't catch the tram to the campus, it meant I had to get out of bed earlier and walk. Being a lazy arsehole, I chose the former.

Plus, at uni there were always people puking up from being drunk, so I think I desensitised myself to the vomming through constant exposure.

⚢

I knew I wanted to study TV and film, so had started off looking for unis offering courses around that and the first one I earmarked was Aberystwyth in Wales. I'd read somewhere that they'd shot the *Harry Potter* movies there, which was a big selling point to me – although I've since found out that this was fake news, so thank God I discounted it as an option before I signed up. Can you imagine me living in Aberystwyth? Me and a load of sheep … not sure how that would have ended, but I'm guessing not well.

I eventually landed on Nottingham Trent because a good friend of mine from home, let's call her Angie, was going there and I thought I might as well copy her. So, I applied to study filmmaking and, for some reason, the fools let me in.

Obviously I was scared about moving away and starting somewhere new, but with Angie at least I would have one familiar face and I told myself I could always drop out if it was completely unbearable.

That was my mindset.

And so, in September 2018, I packed up my pink suitcase and my parents drove to Nottingham where they dropped me off with my teddy Rabbie Williams and promptly abandoned us. And I'm not going to sugarcoat it, when they left me there on that first day, my stomach lurched and I needed to sit down on the single bed with my intrusive thoughts for quite some time. I was sharing the apartment with four other students (including Angie, who hadn't arrived yet) and I could hear two of them in the kitchen so I knew I'd have to pull myself together to go and meet them properly.

And that I should probably do it sooner than, say, next week.

What if they hated me? What if they thought I was the most awkward person alive? How could I make them want to be friends with me?

I decided to go in there and offer them a fag. That's how it used to work pre-vaping, wasn't it? You have a cigarette together, start talking and get to know each other over a cloud of toxic fumes. Innocent times.

So, I trot into the kitchen to find two boys, Faz and Amin, sitting there chatting.

'Hi, I'm Grace. Do either of you want a fag?'

A pause.

'No, thanks,' Faz replies. 'We don't smoke.'

Great. So now I'm fucked because I don't know where we

go from here or what the hell we can talk about. The cigarette was my one and only plan and now I have nothing left.

I try to look casual with a shrug.

'Well, do you want to go out tonight?' I suggest.

'Yeah, we should have pre-drinks here.'

OK, now we had some common ground.

After that, Angie arrived, along with the fifth flatmate, and thank God we all just clicked. If we hadn't all been thrown together in that apartment, I doubt any of us would have ever crossed paths because we were very different people on very different courses. But that was the great thing about uni, it was all about meeting new people who were on your wavelength and those connections made a big place feel less overwhelming and more like home. I'm very happy the five of us found each other, me and Angie ended up living together for all four of my years in Nottingham.

That first night out was the best thing that had ever happened to me, like a proper epiphany, because it was the moment I realised how free I was. I could come home when I wanted, I could drink as much as I liked and there was no one telling me what to do. Back home in the village, there were only a few pubs and everywhere shut at 11pm. In Nottingham, 11pm was generally when the night out would begin and this was a revelation to me.

Freshers' Week consisted of people being obliterated and/or shagging. Everyone got freshers' flu and was so ill by the end of the seven consecutive days of drinking wine, vodka cranberry and tequila shots, they probably needed to be hooked up to a drip.

Heaven.

The Nottingham establishments I should have been barred from

PRYZM, Upper Parliament Street

With its cheese room, R&B floor and House floor, this place was my spiritual home. My fondest memory from there is the time we were given access to the VIP section. I think they could have been done under the Trade Descriptions Act for that title because 'VIP' meant an area separated from the rest of the club only by a thin piece of rope they'd bought at Home Bargains.

Anyway, this particular night me and my mates were dancing with some guys. I was straddling one of them, my dress had ridden up and my actual arsehole was on display. In an entirely separate incident, I managed to lose my phone, which didn't turn up despite an extensive search of the premises, and so now I had to face telling my parents I needed a new mobile. I knew they'd be mad with me if they found out I'd lost it while drunk so I told them I'd been mugged, a lie that backfired quickly when my dad said in that case he was going to call the police, who could check the club's CCTV. If they'd done that, they would have seen exactly what I was up to with the straddling and the arsehole and that would have sent my dad to his grave. So I had to come clean.

In unrelated news, PRYZM has since closed down and we are all the poorer for it. RIP.

Ocean, Greyfriar Gate

The place everyone wanted to be at, but only being part of a university society could secure your entry. I therefore joined the cocktail-making society. Ocean was the pinnacle, the peak, the climax of the student pub crawl, which was always done in fancy dress, and by the time you got there, everyone was annihilated. You'd have sexy schoolgirls, dodgy sailors and nutty professors all going at it. Saucy nuns quite openly getting fingered on the stairs and shagging on the balcony.

The rumour in Nottingham was that the carpet in Ocean once tested positive for chlamydia. Having seen what went down there, I, for one, believe that to be 100 per cent cast-iron true.

INK, Queen Street

An R&B club. I wasn't really an R&B girl, I'm not built for it. I can't twerk, I can't whine – in fact, I remember attempting my first whine on someone in INK and all of my flatmates were creased because I looked like I was having an exorcism.

The stairs were always so slippery that I would fall down them every time, like Bambi on ice, legs everywhere. Dignity has never really been my thing.

Rock City, Talbot Street

This place was where my heart lived and the Cirque du Soul nights were what introduced me to raving. It was where we went on Freedom Day in July 2020 when lockdown restrictions were lifted, the clubs reopened and it was like we'd all been released from an asylum at once. In a way, we actually had. The whole thing sent me off my nut and I was running around the place, literally loving my life, until my friend had to tell me to chill out because I was fist pumping and jumping in the air like I was in a German nightclub, not even trying to be ironic.

That night is still my Roman Empire.

The Gooseberry Bush, Peel Street

A Wetherspoons pub conveniently located close to the university itself where we'd drink in between lectures and then end up sacking off the rest of the day. Many romances were formed here when people got pissed and fell into the trap of shagging a coursemate, which always went Pete Tong because then you had to see them every single day. A girl I was friends with did that and she didn't come into a single lecture for the rest of the year because she was just too embarrassed. She basically screwed her whole future over a shambolic decision taken while drunk in The Gooseberry Bush.

The Golden Fleece, Mansfield Road

This pub has closed down now which is devastating because I had some great times here over the years. They did vegan food, there was a terrace at the top and there were always good vibes. My friend once got off with the DJ who had a moustache that curled up at the ends, making him look like a 40-year-old paedophile, and after that we could never go back because she was so mortified.

⚢

My first-year accommodation was Liberty Point on St Ann's Well Road, the roughest place in Nottingham. It was full of halfway houses for people freshly out of rehab, there was constant crime, stabbings and the whole area was crawling with drug dealers.

Our flat was a slum. I decorated my bedroom with fairy lights and photos of friends back home, but it was giving cess-pit with makeup all over the place, piles of unwashed clothes on the floor and fake tan stains on every surface.

We had a communal kitchen which was totally disgusting and also home to a colony of maggots because no one ever cleaned up. One of the boys (I don't like to name and shame but it was Faz) was the worst by far. He once put a filthy pot in the cupboard under the sink and just left it there and when we found it three months later it had mould growing out of it. I developed a chronic respiratory disease just from looking at it.

For the second year, we moved to a flat on Foxhall Road, although it should really have been called Prostitute Street. This flat had no heating, the windows wouldn't shut, there was rising damp and we'd regularly have the crackheads from upstairs ringing our doorbell.

One time they knocked shouting, 'We're looking for the girls in Flat 5 for a fight.'

It took a hot minute for me and Angie to realise that, oh my God, *we're* the girls in Flat 5. We were stoned at the time (obviously), so it was paranoia central and we had to psych ourselves up to go down and sort it out. That process alone took us about half an hour and by the time we got to the front door they'd given up and gone home.

After that we moved to a place on Exeter Road which was slightly nicer although there was a couple living downstairs who were constantly shagging very loudly right under my room. At both flats, I saw police forensics teams enter neighbouring properties to remove a dead body.

So you get the idea.

But I loved it. For me, uni was like a clean slate. Because I'd lived in such a small place, my parents had driven me everywhere and a lot of the time it felt as if I was living under surveillance. Being somewhere I didn't have loads of people who knew me or anything about my past felt like I'd escaped, and over that first term, I found a confidence I'd never had before. I would happily go into town on my own to get my nails done and I spent significantly less time than usual alone in my bedroom contemplating imminent death.

I stopped overthinking everything and started wearing clothes that I actually liked instead of worrying about the judgement of others because at uni no one cared. I was in this huge melting pot where there were so many different kinds of people from all backgrounds, walks of life and cultures, and I grew into who I was. Not who others wanted me to be or who I thought I should be in order to fit in. It was where I began to figure myself out for the first time.

Best bits about uni

- Partying.
- Independence.
- Free will.
- New friends.
- Not caring (as much).
- Exploring a new city.
- Dressing like a whore and having no one judge you cos, students.

Worst bits about uni

- Actually having to go to uni.
- Finding the discipline to leave the house knowing no one's going to tell you off if you don't.
- Trying not to get arrested – surprisingly difficult at times.
- Complete loss of any kind of risk awareness. A crackhead once came up to me in the street and offered me some of her wine. I accepted, drank out the bottle she'd been swigging from and then had to phone 111 the next day to ask about booking in for a tetanus jab.

One-night stands were a way of life at uni, but they would always leave me in a state of horror the next day. In our house of five, we were all single, most of us were pretty active and it was carnage. Hand on heart, if you lined up in a room the guys I brought back, I wouldn't be able to tell you if it was a yes or a no, that's the level we're talking about here.

However, I would be overcome with embarrassment the morning after the night before, cringing myself into another dimension and beating myself up. That would last about three days and then I'd just go out and do it again. But I did need to draw a line at some point, because the anxiety was hell and STDs exist which I know first-hand to personal cost.

The last one-night stand I ever had was in my fourth year when I was 22 and dressed as a slutty nun, getting off with a guy in Ocean. I took him back to my house and had no recollection of *anything* the next day until my flatmate was like, 'Grace, what the fuck was that?'

'What do you mean?'

'While you were shagging that boy you were chanting "GK Barry".'

Oh my fucking God. I wanted to be deleted from existence. I'm googling how to put myself into witness protection. Even now, every time that memory pops into my brain, it takes a year off my life. From that day on, I sewed up my fanny and never had another one-night stand. I couldn't ever return to Ocean either in case I bumped into this teenager, so it was the end of an era in more ways than one.

My first year at uni life hacks

- Go into student accommodation for the first year rather than finding your own place. There will be much more opportunity to make friends in the student halls.
- Don't stress out if you don't make friends on your course. In my experience it's really common not to, especially if you're on a dossy course like mine where you only have a few lectures a week.

- Don't put pressure on yourself to make mates for life in the first two weeks. Throughout the year, you'll find your people.
- Vodka is now a food group but do try and eat a real meal at least occasionally.
- A bit of homesickness is normal. Ride it out and it will pass.
- Learn to back up your work. Losing a 2,000-word essay is character development you don't need.
- Dump any boyfriend or girlfriend back home. I had friends who were in relationships and I don't think they got to have the full hot mess of a uni experience because they were too busy being coupled up. And they all broke up afterwards so, you know, what a waste.
- Always make sure you have a group of friends or at least one person who you know won't leave you on a night out.
- Or be that friend yourself. Don't put someone in an Uber on their own.

Although I picked up plenty of desperately needed life skills, I didn't learn a thing at university itself. Genuinely, nothing. When Ella and I started vlogging recently, we got one of those specialist Sony cameras and I barely knew how to switch it on, let alone how to operate it, even though that's literally what I did at uni the whole time I was there.

There was a time when I'd thought I might enjoy a career as a camera operator and even did a runner's job for *Doctors* on the BBC where I shadowed all the cameramen. However, no word of a lie, they all stank of BO and I think that's when I tapped out. Not for me.

This doesn't mean that I disliked the course. Far from it. Even though I wasn't very good at any of it and it was the most unserious, ridiculous course ever invented (there were no exams for the entirety of my uni degree which is probably why reprobates like me were able to pass), I loved it.

We went on a group excursion once, all the way to the bright lights of Derby to shoot our final-year films, staying in the middle of nowhere at school-trip accommodation which had tiny bunk beds for six-year-olds. Everyone got food poisoning, it was Arctic-level temperatures of freezing the whole time, I spent the three days walking round with a clipboard and I don't think I shot a single piece of film.

On the last night, the teachers took us all to a pub down a load of back roads, we all got hammered and several people got to know each other a lot better that night which made for a horrifically awkward bus journey home. It was the best trip I've ever been on by a mile.

I got on with all my tutors who massively helped me out because they pitied me for being so rubbish and I'm still in contact with one of them, Phil, who is a total legend. If it wasn't for him, I would never have finished that final-year film which was a story about my fictional short-lived veganism journey. It which made no sense even to me and I was the one who wrote it. It still lurks somewhere in the depths of YouTube for anyone sick enough to want to watch it.

Anyway, shout out to Phil. I should be dedicating this book to him.

I should also pay tribute to Rob Beckett at this point. I was very aware that I was struggling to pass my final year and knew I needed to pull something sweet out the bag otherwise I was going to flunk the whole degree. I found an email for Rob's management and dropped him a line apologising for sounding like a beg but said that I was about to fail my film course and was just wondering if he could do a voiceover for me.

I know, the nerve of me.

I said I'd give him a script, it would take about five seconds of his time and it would definitely save my sorry arse. And he replied saying, 'Yeah, no problem.'

Shut. The. Fuck. Up.

I was gobsmacked and, bless Rob, he kept his word and did that for me. About a year later when the social media stuff was popping off, he messaged and said, 'I've seen you on TikTok, and I swear I helped you a while back ... '

'Rob,' I said, 'you did my uni assignment. You're literally the reason I passed.'

It goes to show that sometimes a bit of cheek can get you a long way. The worst Rob Beckett could have done was ghost me and I'm sure I'd have got over that within five, possibly eight years.

So shoot your shot, guys. Chance your arm. You never know.

What I learned at university

- Rather than being an anxiety-riddled wreck, I'm someone that actually likes being independent and can enjoy my own company.
- How to speak up without fear of looking stupid.
- That, sadly, I am physically incapable of working to a deadline unless I leave everything to the night before and this is a very stressful way to live a life.
- The importance of lining my stomach before a night out. My alcohol tolerance is now up there with people from Newcastle.
- Absolutely nothing about filmmaking.

Because of Covid, I didn't get a graduation ceremony and, frankly, that really pissed me off. There was no way I was ending my university era like that. I wanted another year of drinking irresponsibly and then a proper send-off at the finish line.

So, for no other reason than that, I applied to do a master's in digital marketing, but please don't ask me what the course was about because I would be unable to give you that information. I did not understand it. I do not know how I passed it. My entire dissertation was written with the help of ChatGPT and I couldn't for the life of me tell you what it said because I never read it.

TikTok and the podcast were starting to go well around that time so I was also juggling all that, and trying to explain to a professor that I needed to take the day off because Dani Dyer had invited me to a party never went down terribly well.

I was back and forth to London a lot, which meant I'd end up having to do my uni work on the train and my interest in any of it was zero anyway because now I had another plan, which looked like it was going to develop into something. But I have no regrets about going to uni because they were the greatest years of my life.

On my final night in Nottingham in the summer of 2022 we all went to Cirque du Soul at Rock City and the last song they played was 'We Are Family'. There was mad dancing, confetti guns, big beach balls bouncing about everywhere and it was surprisingly really emotional. I still get an instant serotonin surge just remembering it.

Basically, the moral of my tale is that even if you're thick like me, go to uni if you can. You may not get a job at the end of it and your liver will probably be fighting for its life, but if you throw yourself into it, you will have the best experience ever and come away with brilliant friends and amazing memories.

And your liver will have regenerated by the time you need it for anything again. You can't tell me that's not true.

CHAPTER SEVEN

So Yeah, I'm a Lesbian Now

Living it up in the land of muff

How to spot a lesbian in the wild

(Disclaimer: these are gross generalisations, don't cancel me)

- An undercut or funny-coloured hair
- Pretty girls with a tight, slicked-back bun
- Denim sets
- Jorts
- Adidas Superstars
- Dr. Martens
- A confident aura around other women
- Bulky rings
- Patchwork tattoos

My first lesbian experience, if you can call it that, came at the age of seven. I was having a sleepover at a friend's house and we were doing a bit of play kissing, just messing about, when her mum walked in on us and even though I was obviously too young to have understood, I remember going home the next day feeling so much shame. It was all totally innocent, but I definitely got a sense that what we'd been doing was somehow 'wrong'.

Apart from that one time, I can't say there were any what you might call early signs of being into women and I had nothing else to do with girls in that way until I was at uni when occasionally, while pissed, I'd end up experimenting for a bit of fun. It only ever happened with two or three randoms and when I say 'experimenting' what I mean is 'blackout drunk and a finger'.

Nothing to write home about and I wouldn't even remember it the next day.

I would, however, have major anxiety about it and thank God I didn't know any of the girls to have to ever see them again because I imagine that was probably the worst night of their lives.

Maybe I was too scared to think about being with a woman for real. Perhaps I was subconsciously suppressing those feelings, but not even those drunken encounters made me consider I might be gay. And anyway, judging by the state of my fumbling, I would clearly be the world's shittest lesbian. There was no way I could be one.

So although I often get asked who my 'gay awakening' was, I can't point to anyone who did that for me. I quite enjoyed a bit of Mulan from the Disney cartoon, especially when she chopped her hair off like a bad bitch. I was also a bit taken with Lola the super-glam, lashes-for-days, red and orange lionfish from *Shark Tale*. Fit.

But there weren't any female celebrities I fancied and I never had a crush on any of my friends. I understood gay men and had plenty of them as friends, but I didn't get lesbians at all. Apart from the two girls I told you about earlier who spent every breaktime snogging, I'd never come across any in real life and the only one I knew of in the public eye was Clare Balding (icon).

Representation, visibility, whatever you want to call it, was basically zero and so all I had to go off was this stereotypical image in my head of butch women with undercuts, septum piercings, knuckle tattoos and motorbikes. That's what I thought a lesbian was.

It wasn't until I started going out as a new recruit into the community to the bars in Soho with Ella that I realised we come in many different shapes and sizes and I still get excited when I see two girls walking down the street holding hands.

'Oh my God, look, Ella! Lezzas!'

Lesbo lingo

- **Stem:** Mixes 'stud' with 'femme' – masculine energy but presents more feminine.
- **Masc:** Looks masculine, most likely to have an undercut.
- **Femme:** A proper girly girl lesbian.
- **Lipstick lesbian:** Hyper feminine – makeup, dresses, full glam.
- **Soft masc:** Masculine fashion with softer elements. Think masc in a pastel knitted jumper.

- **Top:** The 'giver'. Would probably wear a strap-on if push came to shove.
- **Touch me not:** Usually tops who don't want anything done back to them at all.
- **Bottom:** The 'receiver' in the bedroom rather than an initiator.
- **Switch:** Not fussy, happy to alternate between top and bottom.
- **Baby gay:** Fledgling lez, newly out and often still unsure about what they want. Terrifying to be in a relationship with because of the risk they'll panic and go back to men.
- **Gold star lesbian:** Only ever been with women, 100 per cent fanny.
- **Pillow princess:** Someone who just lies there having a great time and doesn't lift a finger. Me, basically.

⚢

Ella was my awakening. She introduced me to the land of muff at a time I was, for all sorts of reasons, very open to exploring women and I've never looked back.

It was like a lightbulb moment. Like suddenly experiencing clarity.

This was around the time that I'd had England international footballer Ella Toone on the podcast and told her a shameless lie that I'd recently got into women's football despite never having been remotely interested in the sport. Regardless, I put it out there that I was looking for a woman who played football, who had calves and a ponytail and that if she knew of someone who was in the market for a girlfriend who looked not unlike a praying mantis then they should slide into the DMs.

That was my brief.

Guys, word travels fast in this day and age and little more than a week later, a friend of mine text to say he'd just been on a cruise with a female footballer who he thought fit the whole calves and ponytail bill.

'She's called Ella Rutherford,' he said. 'You should follow her.'

I checked out Ella's Instagram and thought, *Jesus wept.*

Not only was her arse a shelf, she was also completely stunning. Her eyes were incredible, her teeth were amazing, her hair was in the best slicked-back ponytail I'd ever seen. She had the legs, the bum and she looked great in red, the colour of Charlton Athletic, which was her team at the time.

It was like every box was ticked and so, I followed her.

Ella just so happened to be carrying a knee injury and was recovering from the surgery, so she was resting up and permanently on her phone, which meant she saw my follow in real time. She messaged me straight back and said we should meet.

I'm going to be honest with you here, I was fighting a debilitating health issue of my own – a severe case of bacterial vaginosis after one too many days of wearing jeans. I therefore needed to slow this down because what if she wanted to sleep with me the first time we met? Even with the super-strength Canesten, BV takes a while to go, so I kept putting her off and it got to the point where she thought I was just dicking her around.

'Look,' she said, 'you either meet me or we sack this off.'

OK, fine.

Because Ella was injured and still hobbling, we couldn't really go out on a date, so I suggested she came round my house and we'd paint each other on canvas. A bit random, but I thought it would be a funny icebreaker, so I bought a job lot of paint from Amazon and we set a date for the following week.

The day arrives. I've shaved every inch of my body, applied full glam on my face, lathered myself in fake tan, brushed my teeth to within an inch of their lives and triple-layered the deodorant. Ella comes over to mine and we paint each other – fully clothed – and get on so well that she stays the night. I still have those paintings and they are violent.

I must stress that although we shared a bed, we didn't shag that first time (I hadn't needed to do all the usual faff down there after all), but from that day forth, we have lived with each other and that's no lie. You know the old joke about what a lesbian brings to the second date? Answer: a removal van. That's me and Ella.

The way I was immediately obsessed. *Obsessed.* I had a shoot the day after that first date and told everyone at the studio who would listen that I was in love with this woman, news that completely threw them. Admittedly, it had come out of the blue – this girl off Instagram was suddenly the love of my life and we were going to be together forever. I think it gave a few people whiplash and I can see that it must have been giving nervous breakdown.

Ella was slightly cautious too. She knew she was the first girl I'd dated and that made her worried this would turn out to be a phase for me. But I just knew this was it. Meeting her meant something inside me had changed and was never going to shift back.

I loved everything about her. Ella is like my total opposite in all the best ways – she's got a frontal lobe, she can have an argument with someone and win it, she knows what to say if the food she's ordered in a restaurant is undercooked, she's straight to the point and I find that assertiveness very fucking attractive.

I'm someone who overthinks everything, whereas for Ella life is very black and white. When she looks at me and asks why I'm so stressed about the latest minor inconvenience I'm freaking out about, she brings me back from the edge and balances me out. No one else can do that the way she does.

She's also literally the best-looking person I've ever seen in my entire life. I think everyone else is a minger compared to Ella.

The first time I saw her play football was on a stream. By then, she'd signed for Ipswich and the match against Exeter was her debut as well as her first game back after a year out with the knee injury. Ipswich were losing 2–0, Ella comes off the bench with complete confidence and scores two goals to rescue a draw for her new team.

And I was like, 'Let's fucking go. This is sensational.'

Now, I'm no Wayne Rooney. I do not know the offside rule, nor do I have the energy or inclination to find out what it is, but I could see how amazing Ella was and I still can't get enough of how driven she is in her career. She had a very serious injury but was so determined to get back to fitness and return to the game, whereas if that had been me, I'd have said fuck it, I'll find a job where my legs stay intact, thanks all the same.

For me it's only Ella now. She is the full package.

I know people can get hung up on labels and identity, and I mean this with no shade to all my bisexual kings and queens out there, but in my eyes, if I was to say I was bi it would mean I was thinking past Ella. It would suggest I was open to dating a boy in the future and I don't see myself ever dating *anyone* else.

I am, therefore, a lesbian.

Besides, after being with a woman, I don't know how you go back to men. Men really do make me feel quite unwell now. Apart from my dad, they're incredibly annoying, they have no emotional intelligence and are hands down the worst people in relationships. Watching the 'Ask for Angela' boys on *Love Island* is my twice-yearly reminder that the future is female.

Life is just better with a woman.

Dating men versus dating women

Men: Constant worries about them cheating due to them prioritising their dicks at all times.

Women: Tend not to think with their genitalia and therefore carry a lower risk of cheating.

Men: Have to be *told* to do things around the house.

Women: Will automatically chip in with hanging up the washing or unloading the dishwasher without having to be asked.

Men: Make very little attempt to understand why you might be upset or what they may have done to upset you.

Women: Understand your moods and hormones because they feel the same, babe.

Men: The tendency to choose the pub and going out with their boys. You're not invited, btw.

Women: Girls' nights. If you're with a woman and your girlfriend's going out with her friends, you're coming too.

Men: Always doubling down when in the wrong. See also, global wars.

Women: Ability to compromise. If there were more women

world leaders there would literally be no wars. We'd just be out there drinking Prosecco, laughing at the manosphere and generally being iconic.

Men: Put you under the control of the male gaze so you need to try and impress them by going skintight, low-cut and super short.

Women: You can share clothes, dress for yourself and no longer stress about what looks good. Although I do still get my tits out now and again.

Men: The sex is no good. Sorry to say but it's purely for them and most of the time it involves having to fake an orgasm to avoid hurting their ego.

Women: No need to fake it with a woman and I don't think you could anyway because they'd know, wouldn't they?

Coming out to my friends was one thing. Telling my parents was quite another.

I'd wanted to let them know pretty much as soon as I got with Ella. I mean, my dad's cousin Adrian is a drag queen and they both like Clare Balding so we're quite an open-minded family, but I was nervous about how they'd react. They'd heard me talking about this 'Ella' and I probably mentioned her more than most of my other friends so they'd started to get a bit of a clue. For instance, I'd say I was 'staying with my friend Ella tonight,' which they'd clocked was strange because I love my own bed and don't like sleeping out at mates' houses.

So by the time I actually dropped the bombshell, I'd already prepared the ground.

It was on the drive back to the train station after they'd spent the day at mine with Ella that my mum asked the million-dollar question.

'So,' she said, trying to sound matter-of-fact, 'who is Ella?'

'She's my girlfriend.'

It just came out naturally and so in the end there was no big build-up required. Sometimes we overthink things that are actually quite fucking simple.

'OK,' said Mum.

'I really don't care who you're with,' said my dad, 'as long as they're not a dick.'

And that was it. I heard about someone whose parents made her a rainbow cake when she came out which I guess was great that they were so accepting, but is it not a bit excessive? Ideally, we'll get to a stage where it doesn't need to be some dramatic announcement, you just bring home who you're with and no one so much as blinks.

Anyway, my parents didn't bake me a rainbow cake but they were cool about it.

My grandma, however. The first time I took Ella around to see her, I said she was my friend because, come on. My nan was

90-odd. I really didn't care if she was for lesbianism or not, but neither did I want to give her a seizure.

'Who's this little fella then?' she asked, looking Ella up and down.

'No, this is a woman, Grandma. She's my friend Ella.'

'Oh right. What do you do, Ella?'

And Ella said she was a footballer. This information did nothing for my nan who just turned back to me and said, 'So, Grace, when are you going to marry a rich man?'

'Yeah, I don't think that's really for me, Nan.'

A few months later, I was on *Loose Women* and, forgetting that my nan watched that show religiously, I spoke openly about dating a woman. On *Loose*, I'm basically there as the resident young lesbian – we could be talking about Prince Andrew and they'll turn to me and say, 'So, Grace, from a lesbian perspective, how does that make you feel?'

Nan got straight on the phone to my mum.

'Loretta, is Grace a lesbian?'

'Um, yes, she is.'

'Right ... ' said my nan. And then she died, so I fear the news finished her off. At least it wasn't on her mind for long.

Legendary lesbians

- Clare Balding. The Adam and Eve of lezzas.
- England Lionesses: Beth Mead, Lucy Bronze, Leah Williamson.
- Taylor Schilling from *Orange Is the New Black*.
- Sarah Paulson. Living legend.
- Princess Diana. Hear me out. I like to think she might have explored the fanny had she lived. She would definitely have loved Freedom gay club.
- Vicky McClure. Even though she's not a lesbian, she should be.

If you get a fanny flutter when a girl touches your hip, that's an indication you're slightly fruity. Congratulations, I'd say you're probably at least 20 per cent gay. Whatever's going on, experimentation is healthy and I'm a big advocate of a finger in the pie in the name of research. You don't need to be gay or attracted to girls to have a one-off sexual experience with another woman and even if you're dead set on being straight, you should at least try a finger blast, just to be sure.

A lot of my friends are like, 'It's not for me,' but there was a time in my life when I wouldn't have gone anywhere near a vagina that wasn't my own and, well, would you look at me now. I've known women in their fifties get divorced from their husbands and run off with a woman, having had no inkling about liking females before.

Give it a go and then you won't have any lingering regrets on your deathbed.

Minge fear only exists because you're not used to it. I was so scared before shagging Ella for the first time because I really wanted to impress her and sex with a woman was uncharted territory for me. I had to watch a YouTube tutorial about where to put what and, to be honest, I was quite literally stabbing in the dark the first few times. I don't know how enjoyable that was for Ella, but I'd suspect not very.

The eureka moment came when I asked myself, 'What do I do on myself?' because if it worked for me then it probably would for her too. Genius, right?

Reasons why sex with a woman is better

- I'm confident and comfortable to be vocal about what I want and what I don't.
- It's a lot more affectionate.
- The after-cuddles don't feel performative because we are women and therefore both want the spooning.
- No pregnancy scares which is incredible.
- No penis involved, either. How liberating. Awful things.

I kept Ella's identity a secret from my followers at first. It wasn't because I needed to work through how I felt about her or any issues with being gay in general – I knew I would be with her regardless. It was more of a worry about how involved other people were going to get.

After a previous breakup, there had been a fair bit of speculation on socials about why we'd split and I'd hated that because things get so twisted and the truth is lost to fiction. So, I only referred to Ella as 'Eyelashes' on the pod and promised myself that this time I was going to ditch my habit of oversharing, hold back and have a private life. There would be no hard launch.

That lasted, I would say, two weeks because I am useless and have no restraint.

A few people worked out who Eyelashes was, so it was already being discussed online whether I liked it or not and I just thought, fuck it. My whole brand is centred on telling people everything about my life so why was I trying to censor it now? This was such a pivotal moment for me; it felt like I was doing something right and obviously I wanted to talk about it.

So we put it all out there and the response was really good. Maybe it's because my followers are girls and gays, but everyone has been so positive, especially after *I'm a Celeb*, where I spoke about coming out a fair bit. A lot of people got in touch to say the chats I'd had in there had opened up conversations for them or given their parents the tools to deal with it, so I hope I can continue to fly the flag a bit, because I think there's still a perception that it's a bad thing to be gay.

You can be gay, but don't be *too* gay.

You can talk about it, but don't mention it *too* much.

The only time I've ever had a moment where I was made to feel gross was when me and Ella were in Benidorm in the summer of 2024 and we walked past a pub holding hands. The whole place, which was full of mediocre straight men, erupted. They were cheering and jeering, and I can tell you now it wasn't because they were championing gay rights.

One of them shouted, 'What a waste!'

And that, my friends, is why I'm a lesbian.

CHAPTER EIGHT

Friendship Goals

Finding your people,
curating your squad and
playing the generation game

All the reasons why I'm a good friend

- **Free shit.** The amount of stuff I get sent, I'm like Santa Claus to my mates.
- **Gossip.** If you want to know which ex-Love Islander is shagging what former TOWIE, I'm your girl.
- **Humour.** My friends probably never ever laugh when I'm not there and that's a sad thought.
- **Trust.** If a friend tells me something, it will stay secret – I won't tell anyone else apart from the dogs. And Ella. I think that's a fair bargain.

They say that friends are the family you choose and, if you ask me, amen, praise be and hallelujah to that. If you've chosen well, you should have all vacancies covered.

The late-night therapist who's on call at all hours, the truth bomber who's always ready to call out your bullshit, the night-out photographer who knows all the best angles and the resident meme dealer who has an endless supply of Gemma Collins content stored permanently on their phone.

Perhaps most important of all is the lifesaver. This is the friend who, as a seasoned professional of the Big Night Out, will drink the house down but (and this is crucial) *never* throw up, so when you need to do a tactical chunder at 10pm, they'll be the one holding your hair back in that toilet cubicle. Because, my God, they've been there too.

While you're throwing your guts up and contemplating your life choices, the lifesaver will tell you all about the time way back in the depths of 2015 when they were in the trenches, exactly where you are right now. And that's how they know for certain, babes, that you're going to be absolutely fine.

The friend I go to ...

In a crisis: My manager Hannah because she can give me the managerial, serious advice but also the absolutely mental friend advice. Hannah is clinically insane, so I can get two sides of the coin with her and then find the middle ground myself.

For a deep and meaningful: Ella. I know she's my girlfriend, but we're best friends too. She's someone I know I can get deep with because she's like, 'Yeah, let's lap this shit up!'

For a night out: Tom Leech. He loves a mosh pit and is straight but one of the girls. He was once forced to a strip club and wanted to respect the stripper so he referred to her as M'lady while refusing a dance. He'll also always get you a drink from the bar and is never ready to go home which makes for a great night.

To be humbled: My makeup artist Lielle. She is so to the point that sometimes I walk into a room and the first thing she'll say is, 'You need to wax your moustache.' Not even a hello. If I'm ever in the wrong (rare, but it happens), she'll be the one to tell me to shut the fuck up and it's so important to have someone in your corner like that.

For gossip: Elektra Fence. She is always willing to talk about goss and tell me what's going on in the scene. We bonded over loving Prosecco and slagging everyone off that had a pulse, gorge.

For words of wisdom: The Reverend Richard Coles or my *Loose Women* colleague and jungle campmate Jane Moore because she's lived so many lives and she's great at advice.

For a stupid conversation about who would win in a fight between Molly-Mae and Clare Balding and why it's obviously Clare: My hair stylist, Thomas. He'd have so much time for that conversation and would be digging up ancient family trees looking for evidence. He'd find a butch great-grandmother of Molly-Mae's and use that to help form a theory about her fighting credentials. I'm not even joking.

⚢

I know it's controversial to say this, but my ride or dies are mainly the team I work with. And the reason I know it's controversial is because I once posted a video about precisely that and the comments were, quite honestly, fucking wild. I had people lecturing me about how no one could possibly be true friends with their colleagues, these weren't real friendships, blah, blah, blah. But I stand by the fact that my makeup artist Lielle and my manager Hannah are hands down my two best mates in the world.

Sure, I still have my friends from uni and other parts of my life, but we all have our own things going on and although they're still important to me, for a number of reasons we don't (and can't) see each other as much as we used to. For the last three years I've spent more days with Lielle than I haven't and Hannah has looked after me since 2021 when this mad journey began. Both of them know me inside out.

Quite literally, actually. Let's not get into that right now.

But it feels like there's a stigma around all that and not having lifelong friends from your schooldays gets treated as some sort of red flag – a sign you've lost touch with your roots. Like that's a bad thing! I've no interest in being anywhere near my roots. I'm a completely different person to who I was in Year 11, thank Christ for that, and so expecting the friendships I had then to survive into my twenties is a stretch. Sometimes you naturally drift away from people – it doesn't mean you've fallen out or suddenly hate each other, it's just that you're no longer in sync, you don't have the same things in common and you've gone in different directions.

And that's OK. No one should feel guilty about growing apart; it's a normal part of life so it's fine to let it go. As we grow up, the kinds of people we get along with will change. For instance, at college, most of my mates were straight males. Not in a 'pick me' kind of way or like a real-life version of that meme of the girl with loads of sausages in her mouth (IYKYK), but I had a very laddish, take-the-piss sense of humour, which seemed to work best in groups of hetero boys. I also had a fear of girls, a hangover from school and my experience with the populars, and I'd concluded that females just weren't for me.

Females just weren't for me. Lol. Little did I know then the interesting narrative arc to come.

It's only when I started doing TikToks that I had an epiphany and realised that girls were *way* funnier than boys. They're so much smarter with their humour and their comebacks. It's a brains-plus-sass combo and I'm here for it.

No offence if you are one, but when I'm with straight men now, I find them such simple creatures. It takes zero effort to make them laugh and they think the dumbest jokes are hilarious. If one of them whips their dick out and shouts, 'Wahey, helicopter!' that's what counts as edgy.

Women and gay men are my soul people. Women because they just get it and I feel like as a sisterhood we're on the same wavelength. And gay men because they instinctively know how to work a room, they're outrageously funny and they get the quotes – the more niche the better. If I drop a *Ja'mie: Private School Girl* quote, you'd better believe they're finishing that line for me.

Gay men are also brutal truth-tellers, which is ultimately what you need in your life, but it's an honesty that comes with trade-offs. They live for the goss and I'm fully aware that if we were ever to fall out, they'd all be wishing me a painful death.

I can take that, though. Those are the rules.

My friendship must-haves

- **Trust without condition.** Being able to spill anything about stuff I've got going on in my life and knowing it won't be repeated or slip out accidentally.
- **Understanding.** Sometimes my work schedule gets hectic and I can't be as available as I'd like – that doesn't mean I DGAF.
- **Honesty.** Hype me up, sure. But also call me out if I'm being a dick.
- **Dog lover.** That's non-negotiable.
- **A good listener.** I can't be dealing with people who always circle it back to themselves or make everything a competition. Like when you say, 'My dog died yesterday

and I'm devastated,' and they respond, 'Yeah, so I remember when my great-uncle Reg died 11 years ago ... '

- **Laughs.** They have to be funny. I've been friends with some boring people and, dear God, it is hell in there.

Sometimes you have to step back from certain friendships that are no longer serving you.

If it's a best friend, I think they're owed an honest explanation as to why you're cooling it – it's scary to properly put a boundary in place and it feels very final, but when there's no going back it's best not to leave any room for misinterpretation.

The end of a close friendship can be devastating, though, hitting way harder than you might expect. My worst experience of this was with someone I worked with and who I regarded as one of my best friends – we were locked in – but I'd started getting suspicions that someone close to me was selling stories to the newspapers. Not just about my private life but also stupid, no-big-deal stuff, and I had a lot of other people around me telling me this person was behind the leaks. They said I needed to confront them, but I didn't want to believe it, not even as the evidence mounted up.

But the more I thought about it, the whole thing was in keeping with this person's character because they'd betray other people's confidences to me, quite happily sharing tea without flinching, and I suppose it would have been naive to think they weren't gossiping about me as well. If you've got a friend who's giving you everyone else's business, they're probably doing it to you too.

In the end the case against was too strong and I knew I had no choice but to cut ties and end our friendship.

It was the first time I'd experienced a betrayal like that and, not gonna lie, walking away from something that had meant so much to me was completely heartbreaking. I had no idea how painful it would be and it genuinely took me about a year and a half to get over it properly – it was like I'd lost a member of my close family and it hurt like fucking hell.

Ella had to deal with a lot of the fallout because I was so upset that it felt way worse than all the relationship breakups I've had put together. I guess when things turn to shit with a boyfriend or girlfriend and you hate each other, there's a script for it: you unfollow, block, tell yourself it just didn't work out and move on.

But when it's a friend, there's less of a clean ending. It feels more personal, more destabilising and more shocking because it's not something you ever expected to happen. You're just left replaying everything over in your head, wondering why they did that, what you missed, if there was anything you could have done differently. Were they ever really interested in what I had to say? Or were they only listening out for what they could run off with and tell someone else to make some money?

It made me paranoid. Maybe I'd never fully know people's true intentions, no matter how close I thought we were.

To this day, that person still tries to get in touch with me through people we have in common, trying to get them to pass on messages on to me. That alone, for me, crosses so many lines. Maybe you never really know someone until you fall out with them and the way this person has carried on since all this blew up means there's no going back.

I don't want to be like this, but I'm going to find it extremely difficult to let anyone new in. I actually can't see it happening, I'm too bruised from what happened. It's probably going to have to be me, Ella and the dogs until I die.

Dealing with the end of a friendship

- Let it hurt. You lost someone you loved and trusted, you're allowed to feel grief.
- Stop re-reading the texts. That will only keep you stuck.
- Don't be afraid to unfollow or mute if you need to.
- Accept that you can miss them and still not want them back in your life.
- Don't make it about your worth. A friendship ending is not a reflection on who you are unless you're an arsehole.
- Know that while you might always feel sadness, it will get easier.

The Sean Paul accent is making sense now, isn't it? Constantly naked with cornrows – what a life.

First day of school, unaware of the trauma that was about to unfold in those years. God bless.

My mum, brother and grandmother (RIP Grandma, you'd have loved Gay Pride).

In my dad's plane that he later crashed, feeling #blessed I wasn't in it then.

Me and my dad when I went to stay in America with him. Rocking the bob that my stepmum cut for me.

The teeth on it. Thank you, NHS dentistry.

Me when I moved to the UK. I'm now at my religious primary school where people thought I was a gorilla due to my hairy arms.

No notes, just a cute photo. And yes, that is a Nintendo DS (google it).

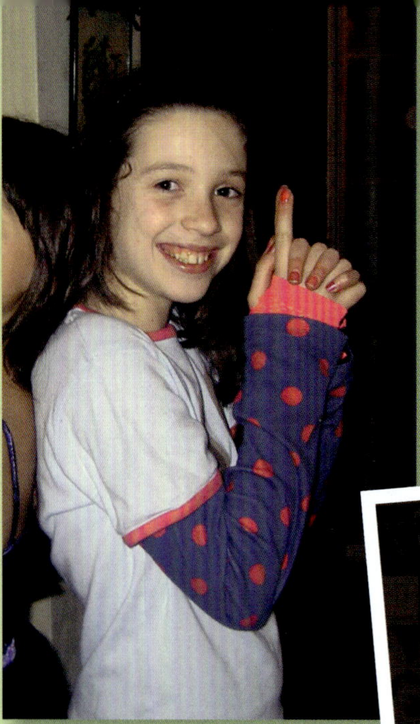

Fashion and teeth are gradually getting worse, but I'm glad to see my audition for James Bond wasn't missed.

The N-Dubz phase was an epidemic.

I was done for drink-driving this golf cart at the age of nine. I'd driven off from my dad so it looked like I was on the loose and going through a hard time. #iconic

Me and my grandad.
He was a skinny legend and
I fear I got that from him.

I needed some Colgate and a balaclava.

Diva.

I remember this swimsuit being so small for me that my flaps basically ate it, so apologies to anyone on that beach.

The day I found out I get seasick.

My mum and dad's wedding. It was the best day ever until they brought out fruitcake as their wedding cake. Blasphemy.

First time visiting my brother after he moved to New York. I nearly got hit by a car five mins before this, lol.

I had a pet peacock called Fred who turned up in our garden one day and never left. He enjoyed cat food and eventually got shot by someone in our village ... allegedly.

My first car – I hit so many other cars and walls with this. If you lived in Mildenhall and had a dent at one point, it was probably me. Sorry.

Example of me taking pictures of myself instead of doing work at Costa.

Covid graduation (aka how can I make a global pandemic about me?)

- Get a dog. You might have to handle a vat of literal shit every day but, dear God, they'll never let you down.

I'm big on having mates right across the generations and don't believe age should be a barrier to friendship. Boomers, Gen X, Millennials and Gen Z can all be very quick to dismiss each other and assume we have nothing in common, but for loads of reasons I've always found myself drawn to making friends with people who are older than me.

When I worked at Costa, there was a guy called Roy. He was 60-odd and we were best mates – me and him would sit and slag everyone off and he was also quite rude to the customers who were arsey with him and I loved that. If I was on a shift with Roy, I'd actively look forward to going to work, which is quite a thing when you're making coffee for pricks all day on barely the minimum wage. We're still in touch from time to time.

I like what older people talk about and how they describe the world and the way they see it. I love it when people have reached a point in their life where they no longer give a shit about all the things they've wasted time worrying about. A lot of my generation moan about how hard life is and I'm not saying we don't have problems to contend with but, guys, come on, compared to growing up 50 years ago, we have it so good. I mean, the severely old people among us have literally been in a world war. I don't think it gets much heavier than that.

Anything heavy that's going on in your life, no matter how weird or niche you think it is, the Boomers have probably gone through it at least ten times over. Love, loss, heartbreak and grief, all of that stuff is human and universal.

Which brings me to The Rev.

Before I went off to film *I'm a Celebrity* in 2024, my mum said, 'Oh my God, one of The Communards is going in as well!'

To which I replied, 'Mum, why are you speaking Spanish?'

She rolled her eyes and played me one of their songs which was quite catchy but not really for me and I gave it no further thought until Richard Coles himself walked into camp, made an innuendo-laden joke and I knew I'd found my person.

Most of our campmates, bless 'em, were very aware we were on telly. Fair enough, they had reputations to protect – each had a line they would never cross and it meant they held themselves back. I, on the other hand, had no such reputation to consider and therefore no line and, maybe because of that, I hadn't formed any majorly close connections. In fact, there were times with the other campmates that I just wanted to go up to them and say, 'Shut the fuck up! I've had four rice grains and three beans, it is 8am and you are singing and dancing! Read the room.'

I was so tired, so hungry and I didn't want to do the paso fucking doble. Or sit around the campfire singing 'Kumbaya'.

But I could never have said that because I would have looked like a lunatic and so I had to compliment them on having such extraordinary energy and then retire to the Bush Telegraph to request the assistance of the psychologist woman. She probably thought I was a bitch from hell as she reminded me to think of this as a job and that when I got out of there, I'd never have to speak to them again.

When The Rev arrived it was like I'd met a kindred spirit.

The first conversation we had was about Victorian children and the best way to die out of all the diseases if you'd lived in that era. I was making dark, horrible jokes (most of them unbroadcastable, tbh) and he was just giving it straight back.

I told him all about my religious past with Jesus boy and the cult camp. We spoke about his raving days and all the drugs he'd taken, the loss of his husband and living through the AIDS epidemic, which I found fascinating. I was mesmerised by the way he talked about life. Whatever he spoke about, he made it so interesting and I just wanted to know everything about him.

And then of course came the scissoring chat. I mean, who knew that me making videos on the internet would mean that one day I'd be sitting in the Australian jungle talking about lesbian sex to a celebrity reverend in front of millions of TV viewers? Not me.

None of us in there knew what was making the final edit for broadcast, although I had a feeling that they were going to show that particular segment, because shortly afterwards, I went into the Bush Telegraph to record my bits to camera and they said, 'Can you speak to us about scissoring?'

And I swear to God, every time I leave the house, I get a comment about scissoring so thanks for that, guys. Obviously, I absolutely adore that for me.

That chat became one of the most talked-about scenes from the series so I'm glad that people enjoyed watching us together and grateful to have The Rev in my life because our friendship has carried on beyond the show. I reckon the fact that we're both gay helped the bonding because each of us sort of 'got' what the other had gone through on some level, but we found each other intriguing for much more than that. He enjoyed my younger-person perspective because he doesn't really have anyone else my age around him and I'd never met anyone like him – a pop star who became a reverend, how mad is that? That's why it works, because we always have something to talk about. He's so old that he's lived a thousand lives and he has so much knowledge, so many stories.

I could listen to him all day.

Generational divides I've clocked

- Vocabulary. Sometimes it's like talking another language. I once said to The Rev that something was 'clapped' and he thought it meant really good (it means ugly).

- Emoji use. Older people have no self-control when it comes to emojis. They're like, 'Oh my God, look at how many different reactions I've got, let's use them all.' If I've done something good, my dad will put about 34 celebration emojis with the face blowing a party horn. One would be plenty. God bless the middle-aged, but if someone my age was doing that, I'd be like, 'You need to get a grip.'

- Extravagant words that I have no idea about for really simple things, like 'stupendous'. I think because older people were caned, they listened and learned more in school. That's probably why we're a thicker generation – we didn't get hit.

- Voicing complaints. If The Rev went to a restaurant and his food was undercooked, he'd say to the waiter, 'My food is raw.' Whereas I would not only eat that food, I'd also tell the staff it was amazing and leave a tip because I'd rather die than ever feel a tiny bit awkward by rocking the boat like that.

- Older people don't have to text their partners all day, every day. They're quite happy seeing them in the morning and when they get in from work in the evening. Whereas if I didn't talk to Ella throughout the day, I'd assume she either hated me or was dead.

- Voice notes. Anyone over the age of 40 is incapable of using them without a Millennial pause at the start followed by some tapping, trying to find the button.

- Inappropriate thumbs-ups. If I text someone to say I'm coming round later and I get a thumbs-up as a reply, I assume that person doesn't want me to bother. To Millennials and older it means, 'Brilliant, see you shortly!' Sometimes I'll write to my dad, 'I had a proper shit day, I literally want to die,' and he'll send the thumbs-up. To him, that means everything's OK. To me, it's like, 'Die, then.'
- Frontal lobes. Mine hasn't come through yet. Maybe it never will.

⚢

Friendships shouldn't be forced or come with pressure to be in touch all the time. Low maintenance does not mean low value.

One of my best mates from school is in a very different place to me in her life right now – she has a baby and she's basically married – which means it's not always possible for her to be in regular touch. Equally, she might not hear from me for a few weeks or months because I don't have a 'normal' job and there's no routine in my life. I love my work, but there are downsides and I've missed nights out, birthdays, hen dos and even weddings because I can't put in for annual leave and head off on my merry way. If I'm filming a TV show, the schedule is the schedule and it can't be bent for me to attend a baby shower.

She understands that because good friends give each other the leeway not to be available all the time.

How not to ghost your friends when you're busy AF

- Don't just disappear. Let them know you're going to be off radar for a while and that it doesn't mean you hate them.
- Book in a date to have lunch or drinks on the other side.
- Drop the odd text – even just a heart emoji to let them know you're still alive.
- Birthdays are key. I've had to miss a lot of birthday nights out, but I don't forget the dates and make sure to send a card or a gift to show I'm thinking of them.

It's been hard to find a balance of giving everyone time when I don't have much of it to go round, but I don't want friendships that are stressy or energy sapping – that's what school was for. I'm more than happy with my no-drama crew, my bubble of good vibes, which is exactly what friendship should be.

CHAPTER NINE

Chronically Online

Scrolling, trolling and the best ever days on the internet

Irritating social media trends that prove we've all lost the fucking plot

Filming yourself crying

Imagine having a full-scale mental breakdown, recording yourself and then posting it for the whole of the internet to see. In what world is that not batshit?

Body positivity influencers showing off forced tummy rolls to be relatable

I'm fine with body positivity but a lot of it is so fake. When I see these people in real life looking normal, it stresses me out because I'm so used to them slumping and contorting into weird angles with their bellies folding over to create a tiny fold.

It doesn't feel right seeing them standing up straight. I'm like, 'Oh my God, is she OK? She hasn't got her trousers undone.'

TikTok shop

When people turn into a telesales person and post videos saying stuff like, 'Someone's getting fired! I can't believe these products are so heavily discounted!' Please shut up. Excuse me but I just can't with the second-hand embarrassment that brings me.

Sunset gazing

Filming yourself on a hill somewhere looking all serious alongside an AI-generated post about the meaning of life/going sober/body confidence. That is horrific.

Fake days in the life

Vlogs that start with the person waking up, stretching and rising out of bed. Guys, do you think we're not all there? We know you've already got up to set up your camera. In fairness, I slag it off but I'll then watch the whole vlog.

Wistful walking shots

Filmed as if they've just strolled all nonchalant past the camera. The reality is they've had to place the camera somewhere, get it into position, do the walk and then run back to check it's been captured correctly. If I saw that happening in real life it would give me the biggest ick.

I imagine life before the internet to be like the Victorian times. People sitting by the fire to keep warm, taking baths in a metal tin, playing out on the street with a hoop and stick and then dying of tuberculosis if not boredom.

Before social media, I don't even know how people interacted with each other. Carrier pigeon? Letters? By the time it's arrived, the gossip you're writing about has surely progressed.

Phone calls? Absolutely not. I could never. If I'd been born in the era of the landline, I would have chosen to be a recluse.

How did people find where anything was without a map to consult on their phone? I remember my parents using paper maps and it almost always resulted in a brutal murder as well as being hopelessly lost. How was it even possible to work out how to use the Tube before the Trainline app existed telling us exactly how to get from King's Cross to Marble Arch? Because I can't see how that worked. The Tube map is an absolute foreign world to me so without the Trainline I would have had to remain in my hometown at all times because I never know where the fuck I'm going.

I'm not just reliant on my phone, I'd say I was in an abusive relationship with it. We all are. If the entire internet was suddenly switched off and we couldn't get online, I'd be licking windows and that's honest to God because I actually wouldn't know what else to do.

I've done two TV shows now where I've had my phone taken from me (*I'm a Celebrity* and *Locked In*) and everyone else on there raved about how lovely it was.

'Oh, isn't this wonderful?' they gush. 'It's like a reset.'

Lunatics and liars.

'No,' I say. 'There's nothing wonderful about this. This is hell. What am I supposed to do now when I'm sitting on the toilet?'

My social network

TikTok

Probably my favourite platform because I can post anything on there unfiltered and people won't question it. TikTok is basically a slum where you can let it all hang out.

Instagram

A bit more bougie. A lot of what I post on TikTok I wouldn't dream of putting on Instagram because I'm more aware of who follows me on there. It's more pristine and about the aesthetic.

Facebook

I'm still on there purely to stalk people I went to school with. It's my favourite to observe who's just checked into hospital or who's getting a divorce and I will sit there and read every one of the 165 comments. Facebook is messy and I love it.

Twitter/X

I had to delete my Twitter before I went into the jungle because I thought there was a risk of my old Jedward fan page being traced and I would have lost all dignity. I do still have a secret Twitter account just for keeping up with what other people are posting and it's a horrible place.

Snapchat

I'm on it but don't speak to anyone, I just like posting stories. At the time of writing, me and Ella have a 435-day streak because we're 16 years of age, apparently.

My screen time is about nine hours a day which is utterly disgusting. If yours is higher than that, tell me and help me hate myself less. I wish I could use 'but it's for work' as an excuse, but I can't because I only actually post once every fortnight on TikTok so the vast majority of those nine hours are spent scrolling through other people's lives, checking out the Facebook statuses from the yummy mummies, losing my mind over traveller girl cleaning videos and watching reality stars doing GRWMs. All while I'm doing fuck all.

I have no boundaries. If I'm not on my phone, I'm playing on the Nintendo Switch, so it's replacing one screen with another.

I get up at 6.30am to let the dogs out and while they're in the garden, I'll open Instagram and have my first scroll of the day before moving on to TikTok. After that, I'll see if I've got any important messages which I'll read and then ignore completely* and once I've got the dogs back in, it's a constant cycle of TikTok, Instagram and watching *Real Housewives* on my phone while attempting to get other shit done.

I can't do housework, cooking or anything without having something playing on my phone because my concentration is shot and my attention span is approximately 30 seconds. I also used to have this obsession where I couldn't sleep unless I'd checked every single social media app to make sure I'd not accidentally posted something and then that became a

---

* I'm someone you will not get a reply from for approximately five business days, if I reply at all. Equally, when I message someone, I'm very happy for them not to reply for several days because that saves me the stress of responding to their reply. Unless it's about gossip in which case I'm going to need a response immediately.

Just so we're all clear.

never-ending cycle of horror. You know you've had too much TikTok for one day when the crackheads are starting to get to it on live – a clear sign if ever there was one that you need to step away from the phone and go to bed.

⚢

If I ditched my phone for a day I would probably come out in hives. I think I'd start shaking, possibly vomiting, and I'd have to return home to retrieve the phone as quickly as possible. I once went on a dog walk without it and that was the quickest dog walk I've ever done in my life. The way I raced home. Sherry-Baby and Noodle were nearly in cardiac arrest from exhaustion when we got back.

But I am trying to use my phone less. When I'm watching a series like *Love Island* I only allow myself to be on it during the ad breaks because a 'little and often, baby steps' approach is more effective for me than trying to go cold turkey like an addict coming off smack.

A girl I used to live with at uni would bang on about how our brains were rotting and she would make a conscious effort not to use her phone, but I knew she was bored shitless without it. I could literally see her sweating and losing the will to live and I didn't know why she was doing that to herself. Just accept it.

I feel I need it on my person at all times because I rely on it for everything. How else would I find out the capital of obscure countries, the names of random actors, the lyrics to songs I can't remember or whether it's true that sloths can hold their breath longer than dolphins? (It is.)

Random shit I regularly google

- What was Henry VIII's shagging chair all about?
- What did Henry VIII eat?
- Did he have gout?
- What is gout?
- Do I have gout?
- How many people are murdered in the UK a year? Just so I can always be on my toes.
- Where can I buy stuff on the black market?
- Have I got dementia?
- What is the best way to kill someone and get away with murder? (Stab them with an icicle because then the murder weapon melts, in case you're interested.)
- Have I got cancer? (I spend at least 15 minutes every evening thinking about how I definitely have stage four of every disease under the sun.)

I feel like we can't discuss social media without mentioning the fact that people have found their voice and decided to be fucking awful to each other. It's given bellends a way of saying nasty shit with no comebacks and if they said what they put online to someone face to face in real life they'd probably get their teeth knocked out. With social media they can do it and then just go about their day feeling great about themselves.

Not to sound like a mum, but if you've ever been trolled, it's usually because they're jealous of something you're doing or something you have that they don't. It's also worth remembering that whenever I've seen trolls unmasked, they look exactly how you'd expect, so take anything they say with a pinch of salt. Unless someone has the bollocks to come and say it to your face, pay no mind about it.

I wouldn't say the hate doesn't ever affect me – a friend of mine was so badly trolled that they had to get the police involved.

I am quite hardened to a lot of it these days and they're more likely to make me laugh than trigger a meltdown. And I actually love *Daily Mail* comments about me most of all because they're so mental.

'How much slap does this chav wear?'

Thank you for noticing; a lot of work went into making up this face.

Generally, I'd say the internet troll falls into one of three camps:

1. There are some irredeemable pricks who get off on it and find it a source of fun being able to say awful stuff with no consequences. Maybe they aren't confrontational in their day-to-day lives, but they can be that person on social media and it makes them feel like Bertie Big Balls for a while.
2. Then there are those who are going through crap in their life and seeing celebrities or influencers appearing to go around without a care in the world causes them to project. So it all stems from their own unhappiness and I get that.
3. And finally there are the ones who are simply young and incredibly stupid. I mean, there's shit I've put on social media back in the day trying to impress people or make them think I was edgy, so whenever I get a comment from a young boy calling me a dyke, I assume he's going through a particularly tricky point in his puberty and this is a phase he will grow out of once he's no longer a massive virgin.

Genuine hate comments I've had on social media

'You've got a flat arse.'
Correct. I do. Apart from making sitting on chairs quite uncomfortable, it doesn't hinder my life.

'You look like a chav.'
Accurate. That was the era I grew up in so we can't hate on it now.

'You're not funny.'
Tell that to the bank.

'Look, Will from *The Inbetweeners* has grown some tits.'
Tits? If only.

'How much makeup do you want to wear?'
All of it. All the makeup in the universe. I want to look like I am airbrushed. I want my pores to be gagging for air at the end of the day. That's my kink.

Clearly, I have no judgement when it comes to what's appropriate to share. At the beginning of doing social media, I genuinely didn't think anyone was ever going to see what I was posting, so I went all in and didn't hold back. The concept of views translating into real human beings didn't compute for me, and even now when it tells me 300,000 people have seen a post, I find it scarily easy to dismiss that figure as just a number.

Don't know who's seen this. Doesn't affect me. I don't care.

However, if you were to put 300,000 actual people in front of me and say that every single one of them had just watched me talking about my vagina, then I would probably require immediate medical assistance.

On the whole, I'd say I'm at peace with every post I've put out. Apart from one. A deeply unwise disclosure that has come back to bite me on the arse again and again.

If I could time travel, I would delete ever saying that I'd contracted chlamydia at uni because that was a diabolical move and I still cannot fathom what in the name of fuckery possessed me to do that. For months afterwards, if you searched my name, the first hit to come up would be 'GK Barry, chlamydia'.

It followed me round for so long (the confession, not the chlamydia – that was gone after a solid seven-day course of antibiotics), it became an act of self-sabotage, constantly throwing me under the bus.

I got an interview to do *Love Island*, which, at the time, was my main goal in life, so I was beside myself that this was my big chance. The first question the casting producer asked was, 'So, what do you do on social media and what sort of content do you post?'

And of all the possible answers I could have given – comedy about my breakups, funny observations about life in general – my brain thought this was the best one.

'I talk about being at uni and, like, having chlamydia.'

The call was terminated shortly after that.

'I don't think you're quite what we're looking for,' said the woman.

And that was the end of my *Love Island* dream.

But I also know there's very little point in me dialling

back the smut and going PG now. It would be different if I was Molly-Mae – if she started talking about STDs and all the people she'd shagged then everyone would be concerned.

'What the fuck is happening with Molly-Mae? Does she need to be sectioned?'

Because I've done that stuff from the start and made a career from putting my life out there, nobody bats an eyelid these days. In fact, when I first got together with Ella, people complained that I'd changed and gone too tame and they didn't like it. So I had to get gastroenteritis and shit myself to put us all back on track.

There's still a balance to strike. There are things I want to keep private or don't want to talk about, so I know to watch myself from time to time and try to bear in mind that sometimes words can have consequences. I did *The Fellas* podcast where I spoke about an ex assuming he would never see or hear of it. Not only did he see it, he got in contact with the hosts Calfreezy and Chip and absolutely went to town on them, so that was a reality check because my family home is still in the area where he lives, which means there's the potential for me bumping into him and when that happens it's going to be extremely awkward.

Similarly, when I slag off the girls from my school, I need to think about the fact that one day there might be an organised reunion where I have to face them and take accountability. And don't try and tell me I could always just not go because when it happens, I am 100 per cent attending that school reunion and I'm going to arrive by helicopter purely to prove a point.

Should I post this?

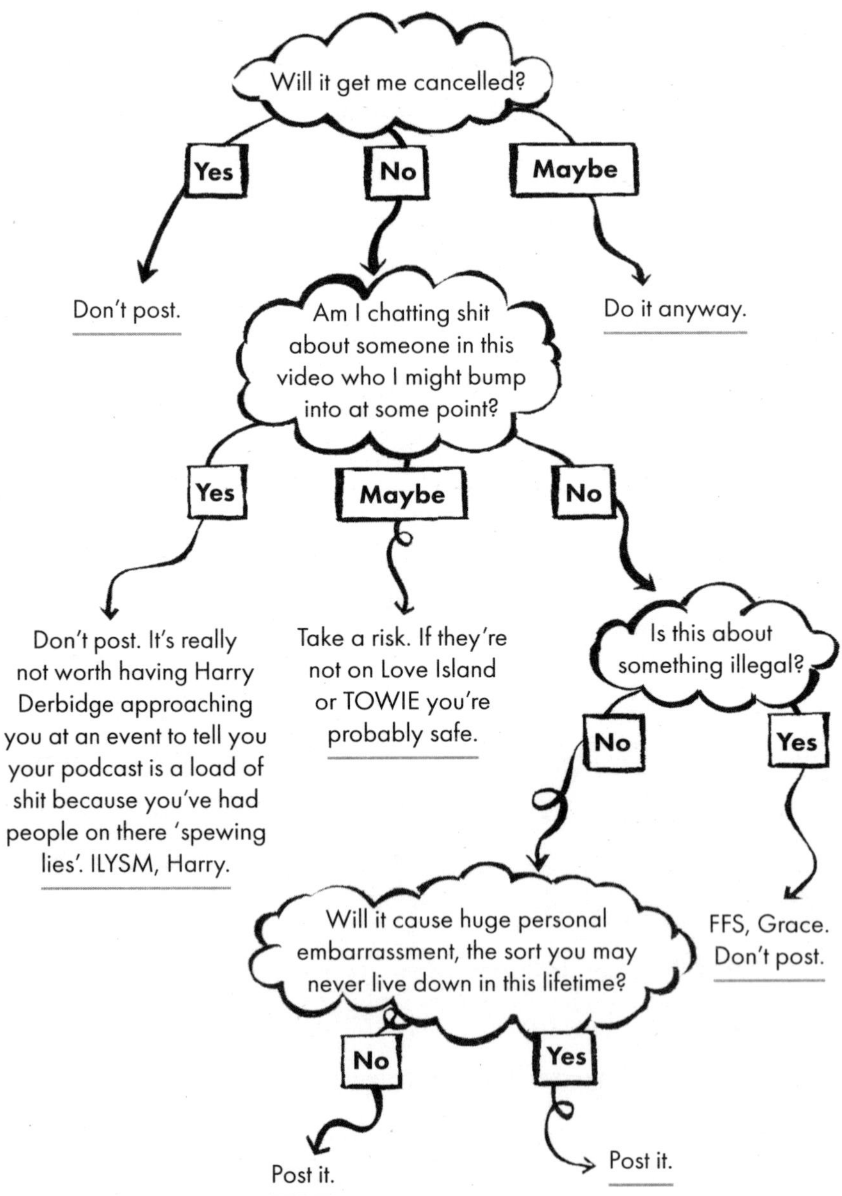

We are way too trusting of what we see on social media. The fake news is out of control and there are creators on TikTok who aren't even journalists, reporting on live news stories which people then take as gospel.

My mum is so guilty of falling for this.

'Have you heard what's happening with Kerry Katona?' she'll say.

'Go on, tell me.'

'Well, she's turned lesbian now.'

'How do you know this, Mum?'

'I read it on Facebook.'

But look, while I'm the first to admit the internet can be brain rot that'll be the ruin of us all, it's also humanity's greatest ever invention and I don't think any of us could live without it. It's given us so many positives – the joy of right-side-of-legal social media stalking, the ability to find answers to absolutely everything and knowledge of huge events within a millisecond of them happening.

Brooklyn Beckham disowning his family.

Wagatha Christie.

When someone famous has popped their clogs, we now know when the body's still warm.

There's no doubt social media needs to be more robustly regulated, especially for kids and teenagers, but for all the dodgy elements, it has revolutionised the way we communicate with each other for the better. I got into Asian TikTok earlier this year and, no exaggeration, that has been life-changing. In the space of a week I'd learned how to make ramen, the cures for every illness in existence and the secrets of the Chinese daily routine which involves drinking a lot of hot water to support gut health. In other words, it helps you take a large shit every morning which is why Chinese people never age and live until they're 145. Cold, hard facts.

And if that isn't worth your monthly broadband bill alone, then I don't know what is.

In celebration of the worldwide web, I give you the greatest days on the internet

Brooklyn Beckham's mic drop

I'm surprised the internet didn't actually break the night Brooklyn put out that 821-word statement, taking down David and Victoria and the House of Beckham across six explosive Instagram stories. A truly extraordinary evening that will live in our hearts and minds forever and saw the nation come together, united by the gossip, the memes and the frenzy that followed. I didn't sleep all night thinking about how Victoria might have danced 'on' him. I still think about it often.

Wagatha Christie

Queen Coleen Rooney's finest hour exposing the guilty party she claimed was leaking stories to the press about her. Her jaw-dropping 'It's …… Rebekah Vardy's account' post came after a highly skilled solo investigation to catch the culprit and led to a multimillion-pound libel trial. Which, of course, my girl Coleen won.

#HasJustineLandedYet

In 2013, the Twitter hashtag tracked the 12-hour flight to South Africa a woman called Justine Sacco had boarded after posting a racist joke about AIDS. With no Wi-Fi on the plane, she had no idea she'd gone viral until she landed in Cape Town to discover that her life had detonated, the internet had collectively cancelled her and she'd been fired from her job. Not a great day for her.

Coldplay's kisscam

If you're having an affair or any sort of secret relationship, maybe don't practically shag at a concert where there's a 60-foot jumbotron and 50,000 camera phones. And if the lens does land on you, probably best to style it out rather than trying to duck out of sight, otherwise you'll become immortalised as a meme.

Kids interrupting their dad's live interview

Remember when that poor guy was being Skype-interviewed on the BBC about something really serious and important, only to have his children burst into the room behind him? The two kids were closely followed by his mortified wife, trousers still round her ankles because she'd been on the loo when the children had made a break for it. Absolute scenes.

***Gemma Collins falling down on* Dancing on Ice**

I'm sorry but this lives rent-free in my head. Love of Huns and Hunsnet went crazy. We should have a national holiday every year for all those who wish to celebrate. The time the GC fell through the stage at the Radio 1 Teen Awards is also up there. What a woman.

J.Lo being rude to Glam Bot

The way she is so ice cold to a guy who is there to make her look good. How he remains so polite to her is next-level impressive.

***Curtis and AJ Pritchard starring on* Hollyoaks**

I will never tire of watching this crime against acting. Those Pritchard boys should not be able to go anywhere for the rest of their lives without someone popping up to say, 'How's Trish?'

***Diane on* The Traitors**

'Paul isn't my son. But Ross is.' No notes. Iconic.

Amy Hart on* Love Island*: 'I was coming back here to tell you that I loved you'

Her line to Curtis (him again) was heartbreaking and fire at the same time and will go down in *Love Island* history. Amy was hurt but she had the last laugh. Standout.

CHAPTER TEN

It's Not That Deep, Babe

How to start giving less of a fuck

I could easily fill the rest of this book with examples of all the times I've done something mortifying and thought my life was over because of it. Like the time I fell over a table at a celeb party, sending drinks flying and bringing an entire event screeching to a halt.

That was a particular low point for me and for about a fortnight afterwards I thought I might physically die from embarrassment.

I'll always be an overthinker and a catastrophiser – my brain is hardwired to jump to the worst possible outcome of any situation and set up camp there. I spent my 21st birthday in a solicitor's office writing a will because I'd developed a bit of a chesty cough and was convinced this was the end for me.

Once I get it into my head that the sky is falling in, no one can tell me otherwise, but I also know I don't help myself. I have a burning need to know what people are saying about me to the point where I will actively seek it out, taking time out of my busy schedule watching *Real Housewives* to see just how awful people are being about me online.

I will search the shit out of my name after I've been on *Loose Women*, which is always a very humbling experience, with comments usually along the lines of how I'm a man in makeup, an awful representation of the younger generation, I'm boring, thick, talk too much, am not in the slightest bit funny, have the wrong opinions about everything we've discussed on the show that day, I look terrible in what I'm wearing, have a big nose and a wonky eye.

I have no idea why I put myself through it or what the psychology behind it is, but it's almost like I use all of that to verify what I already believe. My mum has always said, 'No one thinks that of you, Grace,' but now here we have confirmation that indeed they do, Loretta.

I look for people to back up what I've thought about myself for years and I don't care about all the nice comments, they don't even touch the sides.

I'll also regularly dip into my delightful Tattle thread, especially on the days when I'm already feeling sorry for myself. I know it's not going to make me feel any better but at least when I'm losing the plot, I'll be up to date and in the loop.

Let's say, for example, I think the podcast has gone a bit off the boil and can't shake the feeling there's something missing, I'll take myself to Tattle and, without fail, someone will have the same opinion.

'Does anyone else find Grace's podcast really shit at the minute?'

And bang, there it is, confirmation.

I shouldn't do it because I always feel worse and I'm very aware that if I search my name anywhere, I'm going to find something to be upset about. But I can't not look. It's like listening to sad music when you're already sad, it's going to make you feel worse, but you do it anyway like an act of self-harm.

Story of my life.

Some of the times I've considered faking my own death

- When I accidentally said 'shit' on *Loose Women* and 'fucked it' on Radio 1, thinking my mic was off. Both times I was convinced I was going to lose my job. That fed into my constant paranoia about cancellation and never working again and having to sell the car and then my body to pay the water bill.
- A million and one examples from school like the time I said something not very nice about this girl in a group chat and someone showed her what I'd written. About 26 of the populars started yelling at me in the canteen, followed me outside and then surrounded me in a circle shouting, 'You're clapped,' and I went home that evening and said I could never go to school again. I will laugh at that now but at the time I literally believed my life was over.
- The fallout after I had Bonnie Blue on the podcast (we'll get into this shortly), which felt like I was being cancelled and I couldn't see any way back.
- The time me and Ella did the WSL League Cup draw and got slated for messing about on the livestream and insulting Tottenham Hotspur, which apparently is a criminal offence. Again, more on this later, but I didn't know how I could show my face in public again.

- The day I interviewed an A-lister for TV and she fully side-eyed every question and gave me single-word answers. I told her I'd dressed up as her for a breakup revenge outfit one Halloween and she looked me up and down and said, 'And how did that work for you?' A few minutes in and I was sweating, thinking about everyone in the room watching this car crash happen in slow motion. At the end I asked if she would do a TikTok with me (as we'd agreed with the publicist ahead of the interview) and she said, 'No,' and just walked out. Didn't even say thank you or bye or anything. It was horrific and I thought I would get fired on the spot.

I'm trying to stop turning every little blip into a full-on apocalypse inside my head and instead treating them like messy lessons I can actually take something from. I learned *so* much from the Bonnie Blue shitshow that I should have a certificate and letters after my name, the main takeaway being that everyone is a Grade-A dickhead.

OK, I'm exaggerating. But it was very eye-opening for me because when I was in the thick of this nightmare, a lot of people were nowhere to be seen. Pricks I thought were my friends were making videos about me and the ones who did reach out to check I was OK weren't the people I expected. So it showed that not everyone who you think is in your corner is going to come through for you when the shit hits the fan.

You often don't know who your friends are until you have a moment where you really need people around you and those fuckers aren't there.

I want to lay all this out now because I think enough time has passed to properly reflect on what happened here. Let me take you back to October 2024 when we invited Bonnie Blue to come on the podcast. She was a controversial figure who was in the news and we thought she'd do decent numbers for us – at the time she was one of the biggest names on OnlyFans and had been targeting male university students to sleep with, claiming to have slept with 158 freshers in two weeks.

This was before the 1,000 blokes in a day stunt she did in January 2025 which she was completely slated for, although personally I don't think we talk enough about the men who were queuing up to shag her for ten seconds apiece.

Anyway, the backlash from our podcast conversation was horrendous. I was accused of not challenging her and given hate for platforming such a 'bad influence' on young girls who would now think this sort of behaviour was normal.

I had never intended to 'normalise' it. What Bonnie Blue does is so far from the realms of normal and if I ever have kids of course I wouldn't want that life for my child. I'd tell them they could do anything else. They could even be a goth, just don't do that.

But there were people contacting ITV to pressure them to drop me from the upcoming series of *I'm a Celeb* and it felt like things were spinning out of all control with context-free clips circulating on TikTok which meant things were ripe for misinterpretation.

Clearly, it's my name and my face on the podcast, so no one else was going to suffer the repercussions of this. No one was going to say, 'Ohhh, the producers at the studio fucked up there,' and so, for me, there was no escape. I thought everyone hated me and there were a few days when I didn't want to leave the house.

But here's the thing. Everything died down again, people moved on, other events took over, life returned to normal and no one even mentions it to me now. And after the storm had passed, there were some valuable lessons from what had been a really shitty situation.

I knew I had to be much stronger about saying no – if I don't want to do something, I'm not doing it and I don't care how forcefully anyone argues back. Just because someone else is convinced an idea will be really good doesn't mean I have to go ahead with it.

When you look back later – and this can be applied to all sorts of things from breakups to drunken mistakes – what feels like the universe imploding very rarely actually is. There has been so much I've learned about friendships, relationships and life in general simply from having survived the plot twists. Take a step back and know that usually it's not nearly as deep as you think it is and everything will turn out fine. You're good.

Working through overthink

Brain: 'My life is ruined, I can never recover from this, I must live out my days as a hermit.'

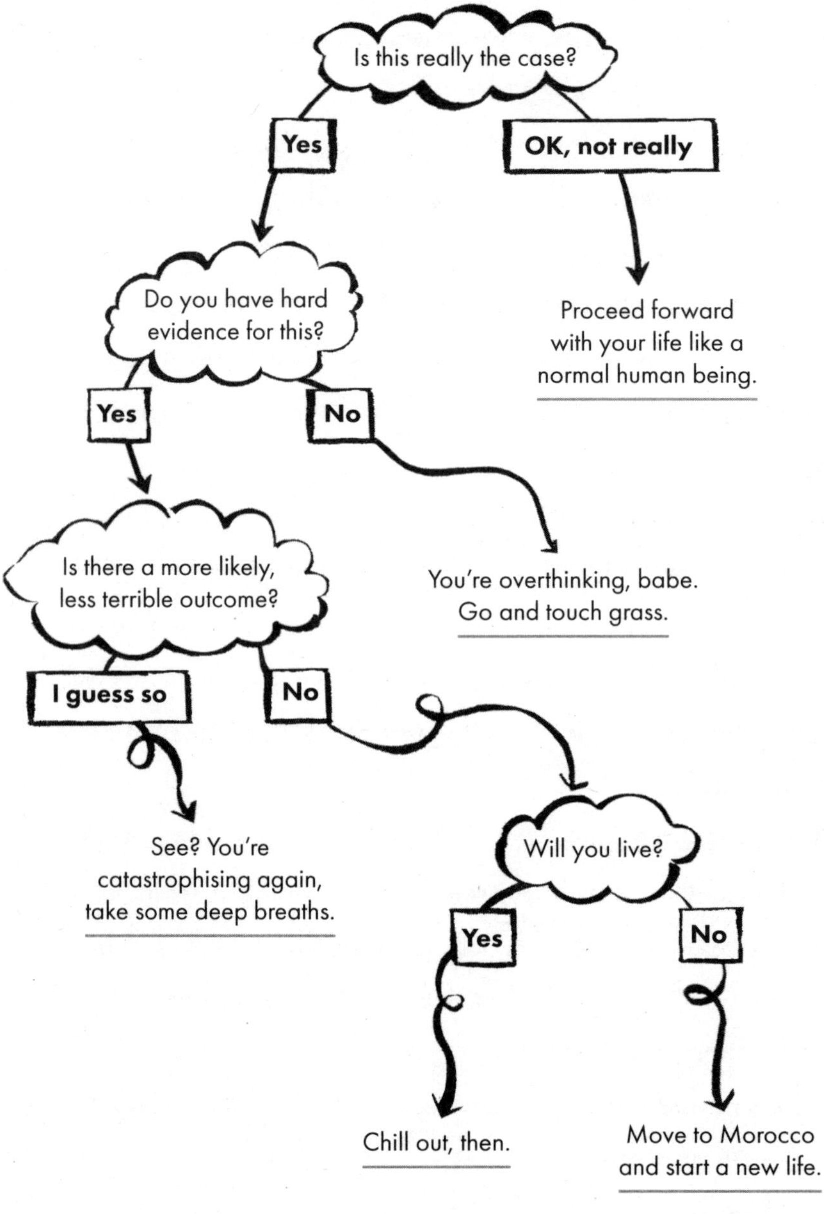

Making mistakes is part of life, even when the ramifications seem horrendous. Obviously in my industry those mistakes are usually very public and so the stakes feel quite high because people like to jump on bandwagons. Some twats are going to join in whatever because it's easy and they don't have a backbone.

The Bonnie Blue experience helped me cope when I found myself at the centre of another 'situation' in November 2025 after me and Ella were hired to do the WSL League Cup draw which was streamed live on TikTok.

I'm not going to beat about the bush [insert your own joke here, lol], it was a shambles. It was complete and utter chaos. HOWEVER, I was paid to do a job where I was hired to be me, and guess what, I fucking did it. I still stand by this.

But the headlines were insane. We'd massively pissed off Spurs (lighten up, guys) and there were reports that the football clubs were considering legal action over the legitimacy of the draw because at one point I'd accidentally dropped a ball back into the bag.

The fallout was definitely giving Bonnie Blue pod, but I was lucky that I was doing it with Ella, because as I told you earlier, whereas I will actively seek out the negative comments, she is someone who goes through life without worrying about what other people think.

I also knew this time, even when I was hanging by a thread, that it would pass. Which it did.

Although maybe in future, if there's a serious job that involves me talking about something I don't really have a clue about, I'll leave it to someone else who does.

Ways to care less

- Things that feel like a big deal now are not going to matter tomorrow, next week or next month. Use the three-month rule. Apart from death, most things will be forgotten in three months' time.

- Keep in mind that anything embarrassing you've said or done will soon be topped by someone else (probably me). So hold tight.

- Social media has made us all very self-obsessed and we think everyone's going to remember every appalling thing we've ever done, when the majority of the time, people are just thinking about the terrible shit they've done. They're not even remotely thinking about the fact that you swung around a pole and a nipple came out.

- Think of the bigger picture. Fear of judgement leads to missed opportunities. There are loads of people I've spoken to who tell me that they kick themselves every day for being too shy or too embarrassed to start out on TikTok.

- Stop comparing yourself to others. There are people you would think look amazing and like they've got it all sorted, but they are the opposite of that. Perfect families who are actually swingers, loved-up couples who are constantly cheating on each other, squeaky-clean TV presenters who are cokeheads – no one has their shit together and it's often just a very carefully controlled media image, so don't assume they've got it sewn up.
- Not everyone has to like you. Throughout life you're going to be some people's cup of tea but not others, which, again, I have struggled with because I have a pathological need to be liked by everyone. But equally I'm not going to die if Susan, 56, watching *Loose Women*, happens to think I'm a talentless bimbo who wears too much makeup.
- Embarrassment isn't a fatal illness. If it was, I'd have been six feet under long ago.
- People judge you on their own insecurities and their criticism isn't an objective view.
- If someone is slagging you off online, just imagine what they look like – I always think of an ogre with a God-awful life and it makes me feel so much better.

I guess there's a sweet spot to hit in all this, a balance where you still give a shit about how you come across, but other people's opinions don't impact on how you live your life or dominate the way you think about everything.

It's fine to care about how you're perceived as long as you're aware of the line where it tips into letting every passing thought from someone else dictate how you act, what you say and how you feel about yourself.

I was a mute at the start of *Loose Women*. It was like someone had removed my batteries and left me incapable of speech, let alone expressing anything resembling an opinion. Even now, when I'm saying anything slightly offbeat, I know there's gonna be a pile-on which I'll force myself to wade through when I get home.

Sometimes my humour doesn't translate. I know, wild, right? Even if what I've said is funny, there will be plenty of people who aren't going to take it as a joke. Some of them are going to assume I'm being deadly serious and think I'm therefore a fucking idiot.

But I know I'm not going to be universally liked and I can (just about) live with that. It's about owning whatever opinion I have that day, however unpopular or deranged it might be, and worrying significantly less about what anyone thinks of it.

Unpopular hills I will die on

- I can't be bothered – and anyone who judges me for it can swivel – to wash new bed linen before sleeping on it. Or new clothes before I wear them. People are so strong on that because 'you don't know who's touched it'. Babe, that's my journey. If I get Norovirus, it's on me.
- Clean-girl aesthetic is performative bullshit and needs to go. I cannot.
- I think we should all hold grudges until the day we die. I think it's healthy. I don't want to be the bigger person. Why have we all of a sudden decided to let things go? That book *The Let Them Theory*? Fuck that. Don't Let Them, that's what I think.
- We need to accept that matcha tastes like shit and we only drink it because it's green, looks like it's good for us and is aesthetically pleasing on Instagram. I've never had a matcha and thought, *Oh, yum*.
- People who stand on the left of escalators need to be locked up.
- There should be a minimum speed limit for walking in city centres and ideally a separate slow and fast lane.
- Assistants in Lush need to stop hounding me for my life story if I've only come in to sniff a bath bomb. If I wanted help, I'd ask for it.

- Children do not belong in first class on the train; that is absolutely insane behaviour from the parents.
- China has really upped its game when it comes to fake designer goods. Shout out to China, you might be using TikTok to spy on us but as far as those snide Dior handbags go, you guys are slaying.

CHAPTER ELEVEN

Adulting

The terrible truth about growing up – send help

Signs that I'm a grown-up now

- When I answer the door and they don't say, 'Are your parents in?'
- Never being asked for ID when I buy a Red Bull or a bottle of wine. Maybe I need to get on the salmon-sperm facials.
- The knowledge that I am now eligible for jail. Terrifying.
- No one says 'you're so cute' or 'bless you' anymore. That hurts.
- Any leeway has evaporated. It's now 'unprofessional' if I ever dare to be ill and need a day off.
- I enjoy a trip to IKEA, Homesense and Home Bargains. If I come home with a potted plant, that's a 10/10 day out for me.
- Watching the news even though I find it all very depressing. Maybe they could spice it up with a quiz or a few games, make it a bit more fun.
- Teenagers to me are the scariest, most intimidating people to walk the earth.
- I make a heart shape using both my whole hands – kids these days only use their forefinger and middle finger which makes it look like they have arthritis.

✿ I got a slow cooker for my birthday and it was the best day of my life. Everything I ever said about my mum's slow-cooked meals, I take back.

When we're younger, we're all in such a hurry to 'grow up'. We think being a grown-up will mean we can do what we want and not have to answer to anyone. If we want to drink wine on the sofa on a Monday night or eat Frosties for dinner then there's no one to stop us or judge.

But when it actually happens and it becomes clear there are water bills to set up and that a TV licence is a thing you have to pay, you realise it's really not all it's cracked up to be.

Fuck this for a laugh. Take me back.

Whether you like it or not, as soon as you move into your own house, you are automatically a grown-up. It is forced upon you. Living by myself for the first time was a proper wake-up call into what it meant to be an adult and after the initial few weeks where I'd swaggered about like a strong, independent single woman, reality kicked in.

What now? Oh, I have to clean this place? I need to remember to put the bins out? And sort out the recycling? What do I do when the dog's been sick? Is it dying? Genuinely, what do I do? Which bit of the washing machine does the fabric softener go into? Check my meter, you say? I don't know where my meter is. Or what it is, for that matter.

Being an adult is just dealing with endless amounts of things that I have absolutely no clue about. If there's a problem with the hot water, you have to do something about it, like call British Gas and actually *speak* to people on the phone.

You can't leave that scented candle and forget about it for someone else to blow out because there's no one else here babe, so you will burn the house down and die alone.

During my first year of living in my own house, I was consistently late in paying all my bills and received two legal letters from British Gas because I would put the reminders they sent to one side and then forget about them.

I still call my parents for every single thing and my mum even has to remind me when my car needs an MOT. When they come round, they bring me food and cleaning products, all the essentials I can't be arsed to buy. My dad built me a shed in the garden to house all the cardboard I don't have room for and they found me my outdoor furniture because I had no idea where to source that or what to do with it.

Setting up a parasol is just not for me.

I mean, some of this is pure laziness rather than incompetence but it's mostly a lethal mix of the two.

I don't want to cast aspersions, but guys, we're getting less and less capable as the generations go on. Tech has done a number on us because we can look everything up at the touch of a button so we don't need to think or solve anything for ourselves. We therefore know absolutely nothing and the everyday life skills are just dying out.

I reckon we need to be taught all this in school; they should make room for it in the curriculum. Let's face it, we could probably sack off chemistry. I dunno about you but I've never had to mix chemicals together to make a random foam explosion in my life.

What they don't tell you about growing up

- Everything costs so much money and, by the way, you're paying for all of it. I now time my showers because my water bill is not to be fucked with.
- You're in charge and for someone like me who is criminally disorganised, that's a huge problem.
- Sometimes you have to get your boiler serviced. What the fuck does that mean? And this will also cost you lots of money.
- If something needs fixing (which is literally all the time), you have to find someone to do it.
- No one cares about your birthday anymore.
- The present haul at Christmas is severely diminished and those who still give you a gift can't be arsed trying

to think of something to buy and will palm you off with vouchers instead. The lack of imagination is insulting.

- People actually pay for a TV licence. Who knew? When I got the letter through, I laughed because surely no one paid for that in this day and age. And then I got threatened with being taken to court which is when I realised OK, people *do* pay it and I coughed up.
- If you have a garden or any kind of outdoor space, you have to look after it. I'd never raked a leaf. In the end I hired a gardener and I know that makes me unrelatable but I'm simply not doing that.
- Apparently, it's no longer appropriate to cry when someone has a go at you for something that was definitely your fault.
- Laundry forever.
- And while we're at it, how the fuck do you fold a fitted sheet?
- Stamp duty. What in the daylight robbery is that?
- You have to book your own doctor's appointments.
- If you don't buy food then there is no food.
- Ditto toilet roll. There's no mum to keep supplies stocked up.

- When you're ill, no one gives a shit. No one. Not even when you're at death's door.
- Cardboard will become the bane of your life. I've had to stop shopping on Amazon because I've reached my human limit with the packaging and I'm no longer emotionally equipped to deal.

As well as general life skills, I could have done with a course on how to handle finances. Obviously I'm self-employed and have to file my own tax returns, but I didn't really understand any of that and thought I could just do a Jimmy Carr.

I mean, haha, how much do they actually check?

'Grace,' said my manager, solemnly. 'They absolutely check.'

This was concerning because I think we can all agree that I wouldn't survive long in prison, so I got myself an accountant and he's shown me how to invest money sensibly and offset my tax through expenses like a company car. Don't ask me to explain how it works – I know as a business you make losses before you make gains, but that's hard for me to grasp because I'm very impulsive and I like to have the money now or just don't bother.

Pensions are another brain melt. When I was with The Rev in the jungle, he kept talking to me about that and I'd think, *This is where you're losing me ...* But apparently more than half of UK adults under the age of 40 (myself included) don't have one. In my head, if I die at 30, what was the point in that? But knowing my luck, I'll live to 95 and be completely fucked.

I'm not wasteful with money, though, and I was actually worse with it when I had less of it. In the days I worked at Costa, I'd get paid about £900 a month and would blow it as soon as it hit my bank account. I became a lot more careful after I started earning decent money through social media, maybe because now I had more to spare I didn't feel the need to spend it all so frivolously so instantly.

Don't get me wrong, I will order three Uber Eats a day and I get sucked into buying ridiculous stuff from TikTok Shop, most of which turns out to be a load of bollocks. Wax melts, cheap clothes, hair tools, giant pickles, the odd bit of minced beef. You could probably buy a spare grandparent on there if you wanted one.

However, I buy cheap so I love Shein and Amazon – basically, anything that's giving sweatshop. I refuse to buy designer handbags or sunglasses, I'll get the fakes. They look exactly the same to me anyway.

I always say that if we ever get broken into, that is going to be the most depressing day ever for the poor bastard burglar, because the haul will be worth about £3.67.

Welcome to my money-saving TED Talk

- If you're self-employed, whatever you get paid, put away 20 per cent into a locked account where you're not tempted to dip into it. Or give it to your mum as long as she's trustworthy and not a kleptomaniac.
- Keep separate accounts – one for bills, one for savings, one for fun/buying shit online.
- Set up a monthly direct debit to that savings account.
- Paying for stuff in cash is easier to keep track of and everything feels like a freebie.
- When you order two outfits just to try the sizes and you return the one that doesn't fit for the refund, you've kind of got the other one for free (OK, that one's girl maths).

One aspect of adulting I've become pretty good at is cooking. I've definitely progressed from the Pot Noodle days at uni and can whip up a meal from scratch without breaking into a cold sweat. This is especially since I've been with Ella because I wanted to impress her in the hope that she'd stay forever and I've realised that my love language is feeding. I am a feeder. There's nothing better than when Ella comes home to a meal I've cooked, and if she likes it, I can sleep well tonight.

Here are a few of my specialities for every occasion. Don't come at me about the quantities because I honestly can't ever be fucked to weigh or measure – my policy is to whack it all in and hope for the best. If anyone reading this gets food poisoning or IBS, speak to my non-existent lawyer and just give me a chance to leave the country before you launch any claim.

Sad and alone green Thai noodles

For when you're depressed and single

Whole head of broccoli, chopped into pieces
Frozen king prawns
Red pepper, sliced
Edamame beans if you're feeling posh
2 carrots, grated into slithery bits
Egg noodles
Can of coconut milk
Thai green curry paste

Shove everything into a big pot, pour your coconut milk in, top up with water so that everything is covered, boil for 15 minutes or until everything is soft. Bob's your uncle and Fanny's your aunt.

Getting laid tacos

For when you're trying to impress someone

2 chicken breasts
Paprika
All-purpose seasoning
Taco seasoning
Cajun seasoning
Tomatoes
½ red onion
Parsley
Lime
Small tortilla wraps
Grated cheese
Sriracha mayo

Chop up your chicken and coat it with the paprika and the all-purpose, taco and Cajun seasonings. Let it sit for a while so it gets flavourful. If that's not a word, it is now.

Chop up your tomatoes, red onion and some parsley, put it all in a bowl, add a bit of salt and lime juice and mix all together.

Cook your chicken in some oil and once it's done, take it out and put on a plate to one side.

Using the same pan, put your wrap in, cook one side, then flip over. On the cooked side, place your chicken, tomato salad mix, grated cheese and sriracha mayo, then fold while cooking the other side.

Serve the wraps and get your cheeks clapped directly afterwards.

No-hangxiety pasta

For lining your stomach before a night out

Penne pasta
Green pesto
Grated cheese
Garlic bread (skip this if you're planning on pulling)

Boil your penne. Again, don't ask me about measurements because I normally make enough to feed a family of ten.

Put your garlic bread in the air fryer at 180°C for 15 minutes.

Once the pasta's boiled, strain the water out, put the pan of pasta back on the hob and mix in the pesto and grated cheese until it's melted.

Put the pasta in a bowl and the garlic bread on a plate and now you're ready to pop your puss at the clurb.

Avoiding death soup

For when you're feeling full of coronavirus

2 celery sticks
2 carrots
2 baking potatoes
Garlic
Turmeric
Paprika
Rosemary, chopped
Thyme, chopped
Parsley, chopped
Bay leaves
2 cans of bone broth
2 chicken breasts
Double cream

Chop up the celery, carrots, baking potatoes and garlic into little pieces, drizzle some oil in a pot and cook them until they soften. Add the turmeric, paprika, rosemary, thyme, parsley and bay leaves, season with salt and pepper, stir and cook through a little.

Add the bone broth and wait for it to boil.

Chuck in the chicken breasts and, when cooked, remove and shred using two forks and then put them back in.

Once everything is soft, add a splash of double cream and any other seasoning you want. Turn the heat off and serve.

Everyone should have a period of living on their own if they can. Getting comfortable with being by yourself is a healthy thing to do and can be really empowering. A friend of mine went through a breakup after being with her boyfriend since the dawn of time and she could not be alone. She was constantly at the office, going out to dinners, doing anything to avoid going home to sit on her own until I told her she needed to bite the bullet and do it.

I eventually convinced her to stay in the house and work from home one day and it snowballed from there. Now she absolutely loves it. She's in a new relationship these days, but she'll only see him on the weekends because she enjoys her own space too much to give it up and I think that's fucking brilliant.

Go and be by yourself, power through the discomfort and I promise you that you'll grow to like it.

Things that please me now I'm a grown-up

- Voting. I'm hardcore into it and think it's a privilege to have that democratic right. I force everyone in my life to do it, even if they're voting Reform.
- Having a day off and therefore the opportunity to steam the floors. Phenomenal.
- And while we're at it, let's watch *This Morning* and have a look at who's having sex with a ghost today.

- A cancelled night out so I can be on the sofa, drinking wine, watching *Britain's Got Talent.*
- Changing the sheets on the bed, spraying it with lavender and then getting into it to rot my little socks off.
- Finding a good laundry detergent mix that makes the clothes smell amazing.
- Lighting a good candle for the living room.
- Deep cleaning the washing machine. And I'm talking taking all the nozzles out, bleaching it, getting rid of the water that smells like arse. Can't beat it.

For all the growing up I've done in my twenties, I'm still very disorganised and I don't think that will ever change. I feel like I take things more seriously, though. I've always had a good work ethic, but whereas in the past I was fine to coast along just doing what made me happy, now I'm very focused on being successful because I can see where it gets you and what it can give you. I didn't used to have any goals. These days I'm very motivated even though I do love to moan about working.

I'm also way more independent and I've been able to push through the anxiety each time it threatens to resurface. I was invited on an amazing brand trip recently, proper once-in-a-lifetime stuff, but it involved getting on a plane by myself which a few years ago would have been unthinkable. I did it and felt invincible after that. If you'd put me in a ring of 50 gorillas, I could have fucked up every single one.

⚢

To all the young people and future legends, if you want my advice, put off growing up for as long as you can. You've literally got half a century to be an adult. Make all the mistakes you want to now and do everything wrong, because apart from being shouted at, there are no real repercussions.

Date multiple people, find the qualities you're looking for in a partner, have fun and party the fucking house down. Because once you've got a career and a mortgage to pay, there's much less time for all that.

For those of us over the age of 25, it's too late and I'm afraid I can't help you.

We're fucked.

CHAPTER TWELVE

On the Job

Career lows, five-year plans and imposter syndrome

Grace Keeling: Curriculum Vitae

Personal statement

- I'm an averagely motivated worker, who is willing to embarrass myself so that others don't have to. This gives me exceptional team-player energy.

- I thrive in social settings, questionable situations and anywhere free drinks are involved and am known for confidently saying, 'Yeah, I can do that,' despite having zero prior experience. I will, nevertheless, somehow pull it out the bag and make it work.

- I'm also very good at buying the rounds which speaks volumes about my commitment to morale and relationship-building.

Education

University: MA in Digital Marketing and BA Film Studies (2:1) – don't ask how

College: Level 3 BTEC in Media

GCSEs: Let's not go there as I find it incredibly triggering

Key skills

- Elite conversationalist aka. chatting shit

- Professional time-filler

- Luring people into a false sense of security so that they overshare
- Ability to lie extremely well
- Working a room like it's a full-time career
- Able to drink to my heart's content and not vomit so therefore a valuable asset at social events and conferences
- Will definitely get the people in even if I bring your brand into disrepute
- Humble from my many years on the frontline at Costa
- Have built an entire career on strategic blagging
- Extensive experience in not knowing what the fuck I'm doing but figuring it out as I go

Interests

Hobbies outside of work include seeing how many BuzzBallz I can do before passing out. So far the record is six. Yes, I know that's very impressive, thanks for noticing.

⚢

I was 15 when I got my first job cleaning my local village hall every Saturday. It smelled like a nursing home and they paid me £10 an hour, which was decent enough although the job description hadn't made clear that it would involve cleaning old men's pubes from the urinals. I simply didn't have the stomach for that.

The number of grey dick hairs was inhumane.

Even just entering those toilets put my mental wellbeing at risk. You would think that by the ages of 60 to 80 (the demographic who used the hall) people might have learned how to sit on a bog seat without getting piss everywhere, but you would be wrong.

At least the sanitary bins were always empty. Small mercies.

The way I circumnavigated these logistical difficulties was to force my mum to come along and do the cleaning for me while I pocketed the money, an arrangement that worked quite successfully for about a year until she came to her senses and said she wasn't going to be my skiv anymore.

So I had to hand my notice in with immediate effect.

My next job was in a local pub where I lasted the grand total of one single day due to being a complete liability. I'm just not built for it, my rightful place is firmly on the other side of the bar and I couldn't pour a pint to save my life. Someone asked for their lager 'topped up' so my solution was to remove the foam and keep filling the pint glass with beer while the customer looked at me like I was an alien who had just landed from outer space.

I'd serve the wine how I would want it, i.e. right to the very rim of the glass, but apparently that's no good for business and you need to measure it. I also didn't understand what a lot of the drinks were. How the fuck am I meant to know how to serve a brandy? This isn't Victorian Britain. So I was constantly having to ask what and where things were.

There were also a lot of creepy men loitering around the place and I'm afraid the whole thing was just not for me. My dad picked me up at the end of my first and only shift and I never returned.

After that, I went to work at the Costa in Mildenhall where I stayed for five years. If you're not familiar with the Costa in Mildenhall then you'll have to take it from me that five years is some staying power. People get less for GBH.

It was one of the most character-building jobs you could ever have – I'd say probably even harder than being sent down the mines as a small child.

Reasons why working there was actually heinous

- I was horrific at making coffees which, unfortunately for both myself and the customers, is a fairly essential skill when you work at Costa.
- My stress levels would be shot through the roof while trying to produce a thousand lattes out of my arse.

- The creepy milkmen who would always try and have a slice of me.
- The iced drinks containing about 700 ingredients, which you'd have to make while there was a queue of aggie customers outside the door on a hot summer's day when the aircon had broken, which was literally all the time.
- When someone ordered with an alternative milk, we were then obliged to go through a massive questionnaire about allergies. Allergies were the bane of my life. If you have an allergy, fuck you.
- My inability to count. I'd ring through the fiver the customer had given me and then they'd suddenly go, 'Oh, I've got the 60p,' as if that was supposed to be in some way helpful to me and I'd go, 'Well, what the fuck does that mean?'
- Having to get up at 3am to open the store on my own, put all the deliveries away myself, set up the coffee and serve alone for the first half-hour. Hell.
- One of the managers was having an affair with a member of staff and they'd go off to the stockroom to get it on. He'd grab her arse behind the counter and it was all completely gross.

My time at Costa taught me an important lesson in how appalling the general public is. They are nasty creatures who are constantly rude, impatient and have no idea how to behave in a public toilet. Some days there would be actual human shit smeared over the walls and period blood on the floor. I once found an empty bottle of wine and a positive pregnancy test in there so God knows what had been occurring in Trap 2 that morning.

Having said all this, I can't exactly lay claim to being employee of the year and I was probably lucky to hang on to the job for as long as I did.

Reasons why I should have been sacked on the spot

- **Stealing.** When the deliveries came in, I'd gift myself a bacon roll, a free drink and a ham and cheese toastie.
- **Spitefulness.** If a customer was rude to me, I would either burn their milk or make their coffee lukewarm purely to ruin their day.
- **Skiving.** Whenever I went to 'clean' the toilets, I'd just spend a good 15 minutes standing there taking selfies and watching YouTube.

For years, throughout school, college and uni, I never knew what I wanted to do as a career. Everyone else seemed dead set on how their futures looked, but not me. I had no ideas. The invited guests at our school careers fair had amounted to the army, someone who had gone to university, a guy who ran an apprenticeship programme and a random girl who came along, sang her own song and did a really slutty dance in hot pants. That was it.

It was hardly surprising that I felt my options were somewhat limited.

I'm not academic. I can't sing, can't dance, can't act, can't draw. I did my school work experience at a hairdresser's and had briefly considered that as a career but soon realised that standing on your feet for hours on end and having to speak to the public just wasn't for me.

So thank God the social media stuff took off because without it I'd probably be selling my body and living on the streets at this stage. Either that or working in a call centre which I probably would have quite enjoyed, sitting down at a desk with my little Post-it notes all colour-coordinated with my pens. Another kink for me.

However, if anyone was ever rude on the phone, that would have triggered an emotional breakdown in me and, since I imagine dickhead customers are a hazard of the job in call centres, I expect I'd have lasted three shifts at the most.

My fantasy jobs

- Wine taster. How incredible would that be? That is my calling.
- A food tester for a president or prime minister – you sample it before he/she does to make sure it's not poisoned. Yes, it might be laced with something that'll kill you, but the chances are it'll be fine and at least you'll die eating the most spectacular cuisine.
- A dog sitter. Unbeatable.
- Mattress tester because you can only do that job properly if you're sleeping for most of it.
- A surgeon because if I can perform miracles people will think I'm God.
- Spot popper or a professional blackhead remover. That's the dream.

When I started on TikTok, it took me a while to figure out what I was going to do on there. I tried a bit of lip syncing to Gemma Collins and a few makeup tutorials just to see what worked, but none of it was flying.

I've always known I can tell a story well and that when I'm in a group of people I'm able to make them laugh, so during the 2020 lockdown I started talking about my breakups, posting short clips about getting sunburned and how the pandemic had made me so ugly that I looked like a meth addict. That's when it started popping off and within a week or so, by the third or fourth video, my following had gone from a few thousand to about 40,000.

OK, so I knew I had an audience and now it was a case of posting more and building on it. Every video I published after that did really well so I carried on in the same vein. I filmed a random bloke out running and joked that I was getting my gym gear on and going jogging as well because I hadn't realised there was a hunk in the neighbourhood. That was an eight-second video but for some reason people loved me objectifying this man and it got hundreds of thousands of views.

There was never a plan to monetise this or make a living from it, mainly because at the time TikTok wasn't putting food on the table for anyone. I just liked the attention, thrived on it, and as soon as I saw one video go viral, I was like, 'How can I keep doing that?'

Call me shallow and I will tell you that you're absolutely correct.

On TikTok, you can get paid per view, but it amounted to about 50p per million views so there wasn't any real money to be made. And if you chose to switch on the Creator Fund (now replaced by the Creator Rewards Program), your views would rapidly drop because the algorithm no longer pushed you. That's basically because they didn't want to pay you and you'll never get all the money anyway because there's something well dodgy going on there with the Chinese government. Don't quote me on that.

Things started to change for me when the legend that is Hannah Holland reached out in 2021.

'I either want to be your mate or I want to manage you because you're just really funny,' she messaged.

'Manager sounds quite cool,' I replied, 'so why not?'

Our first meeting took place over Zoom while she was getting a blow-dry done which was horribly unprofessional of her and I loved it. I thought, *Yeah, I'll stick with you*, and we've been together ever since, both learning as we've gone along because she didn't know her arse from her elbow at the start either.

When Hannah came on board as manager I had about 200K followers but wasn't earning from it and she negotiated some initial advertising deals which started bringing in a bit of cash. If I'm honest, the majority of the jobs in my first year I feel deep regret about and they make me quite nauseous now. Me and Hannah were both navigating this new world and although I never went down the vitamins or flat tummy tea route, I was pushing stuff that I didn't really believe in, shilling for brands I didn't think were all that. I remember extolling the virtues of these magnetic eyelashes that literally didn't work. They were so crap I had to glue them on and yet there I was talking about how amazing they were in the video. It was ridiculous.

But over that first 12 months, we figured it out together and it got to a point where I had to make a decision, because juggling my increasing TikTok commitments with my 12-hour shifts at Costa was becoming tricky. I couldn't exactly go into the shit-smeared toilets and film myself talking about HelloFresh.

So even though social media was bringing in a lot less than my Costa wages, in 2022 I took a risk and decided to quit the day job and give it a go. If nothing else, it was glorious no longer having to get up at the arsecrack of dawn to serve caramel iced whipped lattes and I can tell you that I positively skipped out of the store after my final shift.

It didn't happen overnight but, thankfully, within about six months, I was being given deals which meant I was earning more in a day than I had been in a month at Costa.

I vividly remember the day a brand offered me five grand for one 30-second TikTok and I nearly passed out. The gamble looked like it was paying off.

Making it online

- Find a niche – not easy when the market is so saturated; it feels like everything's been done and there are so many people putting out a lot of the same content. But if you've got an original idea, you will stand out from that crowd.
- Make content that you genuinely love.

- Choose your platforms and prioritise. TikTok will give you the fastest growth and Instagram is best for brand deals and aesthetic content. YouTube is like beating a dead horse unless you already have a following. It's so hard to get views on that platform, because it's not like people stumble across your profile.
- Post multiple times a day so you're constantly out there and the chances are you'll blow up. I was posting three times a day and even when I didn't have anything to say, I'd find something to talk about because if people don't see the first or the second video, they're going to see the third.
- Be consistent with it to give yourself the best shot. Showing up can often be more important than the content itself.
- Having said that, try and build a personality and don't just churn out content for content's sake.
- Don't try and copy anyone because people will see through that and they won't fall for it. You'll be called out.
- Don't be embarrassed. People are always gonna say, 'Who does she think she is?' but you can't let them put you off otherwise this isn't going anywhere.

- Remember, human attention spans no longer exist and therefore you need to use the first three seconds to hook people in.
- Engage. Platforms reward interaction, so reply and react to the comments.
- Keep it simple and don't concern yourself with investing in fancy equipment for now. Your output is more important than the make of your camera.
- Even if it doesn't bang the first time, keep trying. After I'd blown up, things were still quite on the edge and I'd put posts out that didn't pick up as much. You've got to keep going through it, because one day you will bang again.

Content creators might get up in my face about this, but I'm just gonna say it. This career is a piece of piss compared to what normal working people do. While everyone else is out properly grafting, here I am sat at home, making videos, talking about stupid shit and earning the sort of money that has allowed me, in my mid-twenties, to take my parents on holiday to Barbados first class. I mean, the absolute cheek of me.

I personally have no complaints and so, I'm afraid, I do very much judge people online who yap about how it's so difficult and that no one gets how hard it is to be out here at the content-creating coalface.

That's not to say that we don't serve a purpose or we're a load of talentless wankers. OK, some of us are. But getting a million people engaged in a video is a talent. Reading the room and understanding what your followers want is a talent. Enjoying a level of trust with your followers so they invest in you and take you at your word is a talent.

Brands have twigged that no one is watching telly how they used to, so neither are they seeing advertising in the same way. But a content creator with a large, loyal following can make one video that immediately gets two million views and that's two million people engaging with and seeing your product being promoted by someone they trust. Not only that, they can click straight through and buy it there and then.

I'd say I see my name as a business. I'm very aware that when people book me, they're doing so for what they've seen online, so I know I'm there to do a job as that person. I come with an audience that brands want to tap into and I'm used as the middleman.

And the bigger you get, the further your reach, the better the opportunities and the more money companies are willing to pay you. When I was less known, I would get invited to an event, whereas now I'll be paid to attend which is mental.

I now have ongoing relationships with brands and there are retainer contracts up for grabs too which can see you installed in an ambassador role and committed to a certain number of shoots across an extended period. It's all interlinked because that exposure leads to other opportunities plus paid-for telly work and so over time I've built up a very comfortable income from a variety of different revenue streams.

But having a profile comes with a responsibility. I don't regard myself as a role model (I beg of you, don't ever see me as that) but I know I have a certain amount of influence and for me that means being careful about what I promote, endorse or advertise. I have a hard line on not doing anything for scammy products and if a brand is linked to a controversial issue then I have to consider if working with them would be like selling my soul to the devil. It had always been a dream of mine to be in a Christmas advert for a particular brand, but when the offer came in for real, I chose to turn it down because of a political situation I didn't want to be associated with or have my name attached to.

It broke my heart to say no, but it turns out I do have a moral compass, after all.

A typical day in my life

- **6.30am:** Get up, let the dogs out, shower, skincare.
- **8am:** Drive to a brand shoot looking like a sack of shit, mullet out, full horror.
- **10am:** Glam begins while I get briefed on how the day is going to pan out.

- **1pm:** Scramble five minutes to learn any lines.
- **1.30pm:** Shoot some content.
- **2.30pm:** Lunch break. Usually Wagamama's (chicken ramen with extra chicken plus hot honey chicken bites) or Nando's (a fino pitta, charred corn, tender stem broccoli if I'm feeling skinny, mash if not).
- **2.45pm:** If the shoot is going well, I'll have a full-fat Coke. If it's not, I'm getting a Prosecco.
- **3pm:** Glam touch-ups.
- **4pm:** Shoot the rest of the content.
- **6pm:** Finish up and drive for the nine hours it takes to get out of London.
- **Evening:** Catch up with Ella back home, cook dinner, walk the dogs, watch some shit TV.
- **1am:** Bed.

I know I do a good job of looking like my confidence is turned up to 100, but imposter syndrome is a real thing for me and I feel it with every gig I get. Especially on telly.

With social media, I sort of know my worth now, but when it comes to TV I'm always convinced that I'm going to be the least funny person on there and will do a rubbish job.

No one's going to know who I am.

I don't know why I've been booked.

I'm clearly the charity hire.

They've only got me on to pull a few younger viewers in.

This is all just purely to embarrass me.

Someone is going to find me out here.

OK, it's been fun, but I'm out of my depth now.

And before I've even turned up, I've talked myself down.

Sometimes the negative self-talk will get backed up with hard evidence like when I started on *Loose Women* in July 2024 and the audience were like, 'Who the fuck is this? We don't like her.'

Part of my insecurity is down to coming from a social media background which means in some people's eyes there's already a black mark against you. Rightly or wrongly, there's a stigma attached to it and when I'm introduced to someone in the industry as 'a TikToker', I know for a fact they're thinking, *Fucking hell, here we go. What does she even do? A little dance on the app?*

There are people who have worked for years and years to get where they are in television and then here's me, who came up on TikTok talking about body counts and getting arseholed and all of a sudden, I'm on a TV set. It does take the piss a bit.

The imposter syndrome has worsened as I've been booked for more high-profile jobs, because they come with added pressure. When I was asked to be a regular panellist on Paramount's *Am I the A**hole?* presented by Jimmy Carr, I worried about how my humour was going to cross over. People find me funny online but that's because I can make quick edits and turn those videos into something amusing. This was a panel show presented by one of the UK's biggest comedians so how was I even going to stand a chance here?

That self-doubt then became self-fulfilling when we started filming because I was far too nervous to try and edge my way into the conversation which, you got it, made me *not funny* because I wasn't saying anything.

'See?' I told myself. 'You knew you couldn't do it.'

Guys, I cried after each of the first three episodes. There was one point I'd had to hold back the tears when the cameras were still fucking rolling because it felt so hopeless, like I was swimming against the tide. That's when you need good people around you who can blow smoke up your arse and the production team (which was mostly women, by the way, and I think that's significant) came to see me during a break in filming and gave me a pep talk.

They said they believed in me, I'd been hired because I was funny and I just needed to relax and go for it. The thing was, I knew the audience hadn't come to see me and so, in my mind, no one wanted to hear what I had to say, but I had to get over myself and do it. And when I started telling stories and cracking jokes and saw that people were laughing, it gave me the confidence I needed to carry on. I must have done OK in the end because they asked me back for the second series.

But I felt the same insecurities again when I filmed *Celebrity Sabotage* for ITV. I was on that show with Joel Dommett and Sam Thompson who are both so used to TV and being 100 per cent hyper the WHOLE time, but that's just not me. I had a conversation with Joel and said I didn't understand why I was there – I was so unsure about how to play this and didn't feel I was doing enough because I couldn't match the energy of him and Sam.

But he reminded me that I'd been booked *because* I'm glass half empty. My job, along with the legendary Judi Love, was to bring that 'can't be arsed, this is ridiculous' balance.

He said, 'Never doubt why you're here – these guys know exactly who you are and that's why they gave you the job.'

Imposter syndrome can happen to anyone in any walk of life and I've learned that the only way to overcome it is to:

- Accept that some self-doubt is normal.
- Stop comparing yourself to others.
- Share how you're feeling with someone else who can pull you back from the brink
- And then go ahead and do the thing you don't feel worthy of.

Even if you feel like a fraud, it's about talking yourself into the belief that you DO deserve to be here as much as the next person.

And if you open your eyes and take a look around, you'll often realise that everyone else is winging it too.

⚢

I need to get better at taking everything in – things like *I'm a Celeb* are once-in-a-lifetime experiences and I want to learn how to appreciate them in full without imposter syndrome getting in the way.

And there really have been too many pinch-me moments to mention – selling out the London Palladium twice, getting to be a regular panellist on *Loose Women*, finding myself on the red carpet with celebrities who I never speak to but will wet my pants at seeing. I once spotted Martin Freeman while I was queuing for the loo at a King's Trust event – I was off-my-rocker drunk and didn't know what to do other than fully curtsy at him while he looked at me as if I was mad.

I don't take any of this for granted. All my friends are either in graduate-level jobs and struggling to pay their rent in London or they've fucked off to Australia, still with no money but at least they're skint in the sun. I don't know anyone outside my industry who isn't finding it tough financially and I'm aware the jobs market can feel pretty bleak.

It's one of the reasons I'm a big fan of the side hustle and having a plan B bubbling away in the background that could maybe expand into something bigger over time. If you have a hobby or a passion – maybe that's photography, music production, Pilates, fashion, social media or whatever – finding a way to make a living from it is the dream scenario. It takes patience and sometimes you have to play the long game before you can take the leap of faith I did. I didn't start making money from social media for about two years and even now I have the constant fear of falling off. When you're self-employed there's always the risk of someone taking your place.

It's tricky to think too far ahead in this industry because you never quite know how it's going to go, so although we work towards certain goals, my five-year plan is to make as much money as I can and when I've earned enough to live comfortably for the rest of my days, I'll go and live on a farm somewhere with Ella and the dogs.

And if it does all go tits up tomorrow, I guess I'll have to dust off my apron and go on bended knee to Costa to beg for my job back. God help us all.

CHAPTER THIRTEEN

Style Queen

Following trends and fashion faux pas

My day-to-day style is unashamedly lazy. If it's taking more than the bare minimum of effort then I'm going to be questioning whether it's worth the energy and therefore when I'm not on camera for anything, you will find me in little else than a baggy tracksuit.

Either that or gym gear to make it look like I go to the gym when I've actually never set foot in one apart from the time at uni when I entered full of good intentions, realised it was at odds with my version of fun and decided to go home.

I'm also very anti-bra and refuse to wear one, even when I'm on telly, which means I usually have to check if something is a bit too nippy before we start shooting. And on *Loose Women* it usually is.

'It's half 12, Grace. Some people are having their lunch. Put your nipples away.'

My taste in fashion has evolved over the years, thank fuck. Back in the day, I was very goth and wore a lot of black with one truly awful orange jumper that should have been a crime to wear outside. I used to love a choker, skinny ripped jeans, Chelsea boots and low-cut tops to show off my non-existent tits. I longed for a quilted Paul's Boutique coat but was never allowed one because they were too expensive so I had to make do with a parka from Primark. I also had an 'I Love Jedward' jumper and matching bag in bright blue which I'd strut about with, deadly serious. It was too much.

At uni, I stepped things up a notch with long-sleeved tops worn over a body suit and teamed with a pair of culottes. On nights out, I'd go full slag and it was all about the PVC – tight, bright pink dresses that might as well have had 'WHORE' written all over them.

But these days, now I've entered my fossil era, I just like being comfortable and so I will wear tracksuits to the day I die. They hide a multitude of sins and that is what I'm here for.

Fashion trends that offend me personally

- Bomber jackets scare the shit out of me, they make me look like I'm off to an audition for *Grease*.
- Socks with heels can look cool on some and I did try it once for a shoot but I could never ever wear them in public without attracting the attention of the mental health authorities.
- Miu Miu sunglasses look great on everyone else, but when I wear them I look like a sex offender. If you're naturally cool, you can pull them off but that's not me.
- Those pumps that have a hoof at the toe are just fucking weird and I don't get that. Why would you want to look like there's a stable somewhere in the countryside missing a pony?

- There's a girl called Amy Hallimond on Instagram who dresses in really bright colours and clashing prints, mixing and matching whatever she feels like and let me be clear that I think she's awesome. But if I wore that, I'm very aware that I'd look like I was having a schizophrenic break.
- Ballet pumps look very cute on the fashion girlies but do nothing for me. People would be like, 'She must be late for a care in the community ballet class, bless her.'
- Trainer socks. I'm just very against them. I'm fully committed to socks over gym leggings, there's no way I want to get out the ankles I forgot to fake tan.
- Low-rise jeans. Guys, why are we doing this? Because now I'm having to have a green tea for breakfast just so I can get away with them. Bring back the TopShop Joni, that's what I say.
- Varsity jackets. Uncalled for. Get them away from me.
- Trainers with a dress. Wear that if you want and I won't judge you (much). I just don't feel that is my lane.
- Midi dresses. Too demure. I long for the day when it's socially acceptable to dress like slags again.

Before a night out it's like World War Three in our house. I'm putting on outfits, I'm crying, I have nothing to wear, my dressing room looks like it's been bombed and I declare I'm not going (I always end up going). But TikTokers who post about outfits at red carpet events have ruined my life. These people have so much power over me that the only reason I turn up to anything these days is to try and impress them. And if I've worn an outfit that isn't picked up as best dressed or – even worse – someone's done a video saying that I look like shit, I will hate myself.

That's the problem with having a bit of a public profile, all your fashion disasters are out there for everyone to comment on.

For an awards ceremony a few years ago, I was doing a bit of hosting on the red carpet and this young girl messaged me beforehand asking if I'd let her style me. I'd never really used a stylist before, I'd always just done it myself with varying degrees of success, but I thought let's give her a chance. She was just starting out and you know me, anything to help the youth unemployment crisis.

So, I went to her flat and she had a few dresses on a rail but I knew in my heart and soul that none of them were right. I should have thanked her for her time and walked away, however, thanks to my inability to engage in slightly awkward conversations and the constant urge to people-please, I had to make something work.

I picked out the least-worst option – a blue velvet dress – and convinced myself that it might look OK once I had my glam done.

Fuck it.

Guys, it looked bad. It was shoulder padded with a huge slash right across the middle meaning my tits were half out.

My right tit did actually come fully out a couple of times and Vicky Pattison had to pop it back in for me. What a time to be alive.

The next day, everyone was looking at the photos comparing me to Gru from *Despicable Me* and it was hard to argue otherwise. I'll be honest, I've never been able to go near a shoulder pad since.

But the worst thing about this whole story – and this is properly disgusting so if you've just eaten your dinner, maybe skip this bit – is that on the day of the awards when I was putting on the dress, I'd noticed that the crotch of the internal bodysuit was covered in someone else's vaginal discharge. Atrocious. I wore pants as a barrier and then prayed that I didn't catch herpes through the fabric, but all the pictures of that night show me with a traumatised rictus grin because I know what's festering down around my vadge.

The following year at the same event, disaster strikes again. Five minutes before I'm due to go out and host the red carpet, the zip breaks on my dress and I have to be sewn into it – a solution that works well until the end of the night when I realise I have no way of getting out of this thing. I can't do the two-hour Uber ride home wearing it because it's a structured ballgown embellished with sequins, so I tell

Ella she's going to have to unpick the stitching to allow me to change.

But Ella manages to rip the mesh at the back of the dress, leaving it now beyond repair. This is a dress that also needs returning tomorrow in pristine condition otherwise I'm going to be landed with a £30,000 bill.

So now I'm in hell. I'm running through all my options but the only thing I'm coming up with is faking my own death.

The following morning, just before I ordered the canoe to set sail for Panama, I found a local clothes alterations shop and said if there was any way they could fix this dress within 24 hours, I would pay whatever money asked of me. And not only did this angel sent from heaven above mend the dress, he also gave me a discount in return for a picture with him. I know, I'm a jammy bitch. But I'm pretty sure that was a lifetime's worth of luck used up in one go and I'm only running on borrowed existence now.

When the fits were fitting (sometimes I do get it right)

- Pride of Britain, 2025. A black lace backless wedding dress by Galilea which made me feel like the Black Swan. That was iconic.

- The Brits, 2025. This was another black number, strapless with sequin and feather detailing which I couldn't sit down in.
- A pink dogtooth *Legally Blonde*-style two-piece I wore for my 2025 tour. I was obsessed with it.
- On that same tour I also wore a Barbie-pink latex dress which was giving dominatrix.
- I wore a very masc suit with a shirt and tie on *Am I the A**hole?* which made me feel like Alan Sugar with tits, a sensation I enjoyed very much.

I don't splash out on designer clothes but I do like Corteiz, Scuffers and HERA for tracksuits. They're not proper high end although they're still fucking expensive. If I'm going on *Loose Women* or somewhere I have to look nice, I'll order something from Self-Portrait or REVOLVE but I'm mostly a high street girl and love a bit of Zara, Bershka, Mango, River Island and Marks & Spencer which you'd think is for the Boomers but is all too often underrated. And Primark for cheap thongs.

The only non-fake piece of designer I own is a Chanel two-piece skirt and blouse which makes me look like an old maid. This story is so unrelatable, but I was at the airport on my way to my sister-in-law Anna's hen do when I realised I didn't have anything to wear for the night ahead. In a panic, I ran into the Chanel store, grabbed this outfit and bought it, without considering the fact that it was white and probably not the colour to show up in at a hen do when you aren't the bride. I spent an unheard of amount for me but in my defence, I'd been in the champagne bar for quite some time by this point.

And here's the kicker: I've never actually worn it. When I arrived, I checked with Anna if other people were wearing white and she said, 'Absolutely not,' which was fair enough. I'm not in the business of upstaging the bride.

So it's just sitting there in my wardrobe gathering dust.

My style icons

- **Kylie Jenner**, no doubt about it.
- **Olivia Neill** minus the inexplicable hoof shoes.
- **Matilda Draper** from *Love Island*, love her take on streetwear.
- **Nella Rose** has had this amazing glow-up and looks so cool.
- **Amy Hallimond** for taking risks and always looking amazing.
- **Mariam Musa** who does these great GRWMs on TikTok. I've bought entire outfits within seconds of watching because of her videos.

I'd never claim to be a fashion guru, but my top tip would be to ignore the trends and just wear what makes you feel confident. For inspo, rather than checking out the catwalks, look at people with a similar body type to yourself and see what looks good on them. I've learned the hard way that stuff others look amazing in often makes me look like a Before photo.

- Show off your best feature, don't hide it away. If you've got a great set of legs, get 'em out.
- If you're tall like me (I'm five foot ten), don't be afraid of a crippling heel. When I was younger, I thought I shouldn't ever wear high heels, because I'd look like a man in a wig. Older, wiser people would tell me I had a model figure and I needed to embrace that, but I wouldn't have it and to this day I have a hunchback from trying to blend in, so that worked out well for me.
- Have a fashion failsafe always ready. Mine is a long maxi skirt and a matching bandeau top so if it's all gone wrong, I can look demure but also ready for a night out. Perfect.
- You do you. Even if that means wearing Crocs. Although I do want to put it out there that my own pair were #gifted and I only wear them for taking out the bins.

CHAPTER FOURTEEN

Beauty and the Beast

Adult acne, facial tweakments and hair scares

My beauty icons

- **Jordan Lipscombe**, the OG UK makeup girl. She slaps it on, overdoes the blush and I love it.
- **Rachel Leary**. She completely transforms herself but makes it look so simple. Makeup is a full-on slog for me.
- **Jamie Genevieve** who I used to watch when I was younger. Her makeup is always totally immaculate.

Let's be clear, if you have naturally great skin that never breaks out into spots, blemishes or random attacks of hormonal acne then you're an arsehole and I hate you.

How dare you?

I've always had problem skin. Throughout my teens and even now as an adult it will choose to flare up without warning and ruin my life and so there's nothing that pisses me off more than seeing genetically gifted people with flawless complexions. And you can bet your life these are the people who get one tiny spot and go, 'Oh my God, like, my acne is really bad.'

Seriously, it's called fuck off and it's located over there.

My acne is linked to hormones and diet but it will always take an awful turn in the direction of total oblivion from October until about April. The vitamin D over the summer months seems to help, but either side of that I've had to accept there are going to be days where I look like a medieval peasant with the plague.

As a teenager, my skin was under constant attack from spots and I became extremely self-conscious of it, wearing lorryloads of makeup to try and cover up, but even when I'd slapped on enough Maybelline Dream Matte Mousse to choke a horse, the bumpy texture of the acne was still visible and sometimes looked even worse. I was also dreadful when it came to removing any makeup so that was an endless cycle of trauma for my skin.

I actually wasn't ever picked on for it (there were so many other avenues of humiliation for my schoolmates to choose from) but I was hyper aware of it all the time. And it was quite a lonely place to be because you never saw anyone on telly or social media with bad skin.

I have to say though – and you know that I generally don't cut men much slack because they are rarely on the back foot with anything – but this is one area where I do think they have it harder than women. There were boys at my school who didn't just have acne all over their face, it was down their necks as well and it looked savagely painful.

Some of those poor bastards also had back-ne, so against all my usual instincts, here's a shout out to my kings because I acknowledge that this is a journey for you.

Things I tried that didn't work

- Toothpaste overnight on the individual spots.
- Sudocrem – not only did it fail to work, it made the issue much worse.
- Scrubbing my face with exfoliators until it nearly bled.
- Praying to a God I don't believe in.
- Moisturiser with added vitamin C.
- Prescription steroid cream from the GP.
- Popping them (still an avid popper now. It's become part of the problem at this point).
- An African clay mask bought from a witch on Etsy because I thought witches would probably know how to cure acne. Spoiler: she didn't. I'm still unsure as to what I put on my face, could have been human shit for all I know.

There's something embarrassing about having spots as an adult. It's like, shouldn't you have grown out of this by now? It feels wrong, it feels childish. Sometimes I imagine having kids and being known as the mum at drop-off who has acne. I have to be known for something else, please God it can't be that.

When I first got together with Ella, I would sleep in my full makeup because I didn't want to take it off and have her think, *Fucking hell, look at the state of this girl's skin*.

She brought the weirdness of that up first.

'Grace, why are you sleeping in your makeup? That's really odd.'

I had to concede it was and that going to bed with a full beat on my face did make me look like a bit of a tramp. I told her I just had really bad skin and looked so different without makeup that I didn't think it was possible for her to fancy me without it.

'I've literally watched your TikToks and you don't wear makeup on there,' she said. 'I've seen you without it.'

This was true. I'd been posting on TikTok with no makeup on from the beginning mainly because it made me funnier. Pretty people aren't funny, that's a scientific fact and I won't be swayed on it. When you're fit you don't have anything to be self-deprecating about.

How many models-slash-comedians do you know?

Exactly.

Going makeup-free online has always worked for me because if I show arguably the ugliest side of me on TikTok to the point where I've not even brushed my teeth, then public opinion can only go up when they see me with full glam. See, there's a method to the madness.

However, the thing I was most stressed about going on *I'm a Celebrity* (after the plane journey) was having to be permanently on camera without any makeup. And at the start of filming I was aware that my skin had drastically worsened as I withdrew from sugar, salt and caffeine.

Fuck.

Not only was I dressed in these tragic red shorts while my hair was in dishevelled plaits, now my acne was horrific too. Life actually couldn't get any worse.

But after that, I kind of settled into it and funnily enough, doing that show proved to be a bit of a pivotal moment for me. Because there were no mirrors, for the 23 days I was in there I couldn't assess how bad or otherwise my skin was and so I stopped thinking about it.

I didn't realise until I was voted out that it had become such a talking point on the outside, and although the comments at the beginning had been about how bad my skin was, by the end people were saying how much it had improved. That's the rice and beans diet for you.

I don't expect anyone to find my acne attractive, but I do think it's a positive thing to see people with their natural skin because that felt so rare to me growing up and it's taken me a long time to get here.

Right now, I don't give a shiny shit. I really, honestly do not care. People *expect* to see all sides of me, so I'm fine with it.

What has actually worked for me

- Cutting out Prosecco which is full of sugar and replacing it with vodka and lime which is basically water. I'd like to say I'm someone who drinks loads of actual water and is really hydrated. But that would be a lie. I'm like a prune.

- Anua Soothing Pads. I use them when my skin is really angry to reduce the redness and they are incredible.
- Always taking off my makeup. Even if I'm obliterated drunk, I will be cleansing my face.
- Obagi products which were recommended to me by Megan Barton-Hanson from *Love Island* after I put a story out asking for help. I got hold of their foam cleanser, acne and pore treatments as well as the hydrating moisturiser and in the first week, it literally peeled off my skin. I was shedding like a lizard, but after a few weeks I was left with skin like glass. It was the best it had ever been. Disgustingly expensive but also God's work.
- Acceptance. When I arrive at shoots with no makeup on, no one has ever commented on my skin and over time it's become less and less important to me.

My makeup in 2016

- A mixture between goth and 'I like doing acid on the weekend' vibes.
- Full Amy Winehouse long eyeliner wing.
- An obscenely dark lip.

- Cut crease the shit out of the eye makeup – applying a darker eyeshadow along the natural fold of the eyelid and a lighter shade below the crease.
- Colourful eyeshadow – yellow, green and blue were my staples. Think Jessie off *The Traitors*.
- A violent amount of bronzer. Blush wasn't a thing, the goal was just to be orange all over.

My makeup in 2026

- Slap it all on, the total antithesis of the clean-girl aesthetic – the goal is still to be orange.
- Charlotte Tilbury Airbrush Flawless Foundation gives really full coverage. It's like cement.
- Wearing the lipliner down to the stump. I'm not getting filler so you'd better believe we're overlining.
- By Terry Tea to Tan Face and Body is amazing for making me look not dead.
- Huda Beauty powder because I have disgustingly oily skin.
- Milk Makeup Hydro Grip Setting Spray.
- Hourglass Vanish Airbrush concealer. If you've got spots, this is the only thing that will cover them.

When it comes to beauty I veer between four hours in the makeup chair and death not even warmed up. There's literally no in between.

I always have my nails done – acrylics until I was a lesbian but I had to let that one go because I couldn't be puncturing Ella. I'm a gel girl now and never stray from my white tips, although I hate the actual process of getting them done because it makes me feel the same way I get with supermarkets – over-stimulated, sick, hot. I can't use my hands so there's nothing saving me from this and there's also a woman scrubbing my foot with a cheese grater while I feel an enormous sense of shame about the state of my trotters.

I don't know what my normal toenails look like anymore. I've not seen them now for several years.

Other than that, I'm pretty low maintenance. Me and Ella will have what she likes to call 'slow mornings' where we'll do our LED masks and skincare, and if I've done all that, I feel like I've vaguely got my life together.

I once went through a self-care phase where I'd book myself in for regular massages, but I stopped that when I was assaulted once too often. One place I went to in Ibiza, the masseuse pinged my thong and spanked me with her bare palm, which felt unnecessary.

Another time I went with Ella for a couples' massage where the door locked which should have been the first red flag. So now we're lying face down on side-by-side beds and this woman gets on her knees on top of me and stretches us both out by the arms at the same time.

It looked like we were doing some sort of kinky torture game in an S&M basement and, needless to say, they have not received our custom again.

My skincare heroes

- I adore an eye patch. I don't have brand loyalty, I love them all.
- My ZIIP Halo electric skin tool which works like gua sha and is incredible.
- The Shark glow mask to make me look a bit more alive – I was gifted one that Ella nicked and then replaced as my Christmas present.
- Medik8 anti-wrinkle serum on the daily because apparently you've got to start this shit early.
- Obagi stuff, obviously.
- I always wear an SPF in the day of Factor 50 on account of having ginger skin.

As I write this I'm on a hair journey which, I believe, is now the law for all content creators.

Basically, my hair was fucked from years of intense bleaching and not using a heat protector and so I decided to ditch my extensions for a while to give everything a bit of a break. When you've had extensions in for as many years as I'd had, finally being able to scratch an itch on your head unhindered is close to orgasmic.

Doing a slicked-back bun without any bumps is life-changing.

And being able to wash it properly – oh my God! Trying to wash with extensions is an absolute violation because you can't get into the nooks and crannies. On *I'm a Celeb* I was trying to wash fish guts out and my hair still stank of them two weeks after leaving the jungle.

Even just drying your hair with extensions is something you have to mentally prepare for, and because I'm so lazy, I would wait until my tapes were hanging down to my ears before getting them re-done. My hairdresser would be in despair.

'Grace, I literally can't work with this, because not being rude but what the fuck have you done to your hair?'

Around the time I had them taken out for good, an Australian brand called Bouf contacted me about their hair-growth product, asking me to use it for a month and only promote it if I thought it actually worked. Within two or three weeks, everyone was noticing how thick my hair was. I'd wake up in the morning looking like a lion there was so much of it, so it has completely changed the game and I don't think I'll go back to extensions now. God bless my glam team who can put clip-pings in for shoots.

Top beauty hacks

- Pressed powder before loose powder. Then wipe the loose powder away and set it again with pressed.
- If you're not someone who likes to wear eyeshadow, use bronzer on the lid for a bit more depth and it will draw people to your eye.
- Don't be frightened to do a nude lip – bring back the foundation lip, I say.
- Heat your eyelash curlers with the hairdryer for a few seconds before using them and lashes will stay curled for longer.
- Talc on your pulse points before spraying perfume will give scent staying power.
- Multi-use your lipstick as blush.
- Set your lip liner with powder to make it last longer.
- White or nude liner in your waterline will make eyes bigger and more awake.
- When overlining your lips, only do so slightly over the cupid's bow to make your pout appear plumper.

- Setting spray sandwich – use before, during and after each makeup step.
- If you've over-powdered, use a skincare mist and it will melt the excess away.
- Apply eyeliner to the inside of the upper lid to make lashes look fuller.
- Tatti Lashes Angel Energy all day, every day. I've got upside down eyes with really long bottom lashes and really short on top so if I only put mascara on, it looks like someone has flipped my eyes round. It's not right.
- I only use the NYX Epic Ink Liner because it's like a pen. I don't fuck about with the ones that are like a paint brush, I need a steady hand.

I'm a very impulsive person and everything I've ever had done to my body I've regretted. Like the tattoo on my right arm of red mushrooms and a fairy with her tits out.

I wasn't even on drugs when I got that.

I was in my fourth year of uni and it was to cover up another one I'd had done when I was 18 of a moon with some bits hanging down that looked like saggy breasts. So all in all, this was a lesson in how you can always make a terrible situation much, much worse.

I'd seen some really cute fairy tattoos and told the tattooist I wanted this cover-up to be 'mystical' so she went away to work on a design and a week later, I was in the chair as she was showing me what she'd created with the mushrooms and topless fairies.

For some reason, 'No fucking way are you tattooing that on my arm. Thank you and goodbye, you absolute lunatic,' came out of my mouth as, 'That's amazing. Do that.'

It took five hours and I hated it. I tried to convince myself that it might not look quite as psychotic once it was done but it actually looked even worse than I'd feared. I remember crying in the uni library afterwards because I had my assignment due that evening but all I could think about were these red mushrooms and fairy tits that were now permanently inked on my arm.

Guys, it was a dark point in my life. The whole experience made me go off and do magic mushrooms for the first time because maybe that experience would give the 'artwork' some deeper retrospective meaning. Obviously it didn't but I had a great time nonetheless.

I've thought about getting laser surgery, but it takes so long and it's not even guaranteed to get rid of it, so unfortunately I think I've made my bed of red mushrooms and I'm going to have to lie in it.

The reason I'm telling you this is because I use it as an example of why not to mess around with tweakments to my face. I always wanted a nose job and there was a time when I would have been on the first flight to Turkey if I'd had the money. But as I've grown up, I've come to quite like my nose. This is going to sound really morbid but I'll just say it. I've inherited my mum's nose and I think when she dies if I'd had a rhinoplasty it would be like the only thing I had left of her was gone.

Loads of my friends are properly into the Botox and lip filler and they all look stunning, I'm not denying that. But I don't think there are enough people on social media who have had nothing done or who are ageing like they're supposed to, so I do feel a little bit of a responsibility as someone out here who has always said 'I don't give a fuck' that I should stick to that. Getting Botox wouldn't be on brand for me.

I'm a very expressive person but nobody's face tells you how they're feeling anymore. One of my friends has so much Botox that I can't tell when she's pissed off with me because literally nothing moves.

'Thank you so much, darling,' is her answer to that because it's the ultimate compliment to her.

I also have a phobia of needles and I'm too much of a hypochondriac to be putting any poison into my body apart from the copious amounts of alcohol I consume on a regular basis.

There was a time when people on telly first started getting Botox and fillers and the consensus was that they looked at best slightly weird and at worst completely terrifying. Now everyone looks like that so it's normal to be chiselled from the filler, frozen from the Botox and with Turkey teeth that are Rylan white, so bright they'll blind you if you look directly at them for too long. That whole look has become the beauty standard.

I walk into an event these days and I can't tell the difference between a lot of the people there because they've all been to see Dr Motox, the guy who's doing every influencer's aesthetics in return for a grid post.

If it makes them happy and boosts their confidence then I'm all for it. I still think there's a charm in individuality and everyone looking a bit different though, so I'm happy to stay the way I was born for now.

I say 'for now' because I am a notoriously fickle bitch and also prone to hypocrisy, so give it a few years and I'll probably be lifted, stretched, pulled and held together only by tit tape.

CHAPTER FIFTEEN

Icons Only

Discovering your identity and being unapologetically you

How to be iconic

- Be outspoken about what you believe in. Such as not doing anal. I don't know a single girl who's had a good time doing that and lived to tell the tale.
- Stop trying to be liked by everyone, it's an impossibility.
- Be happy to live in your own filth. It's OK not to shower and to stay in your pyjamas on your days off. It's OK not to do Pilates. If you're a bit of a slob, know that this also means you're an icon.
- Ugliness when you're younger is a growth arc that leads to icon status. If you are clapped as a teen, I guarantee you're going to be an icon when you get older.
- Know your quotes. If I say, 'Sit back down,' you've got to be able to respond, 'I'm sat' (Olivia Attwood). If I say, 'Because I love the cocaine more than I love the kids at the moment,' you *have* to come back with, 'And that's the bottom line, Jeremy.' If you can't finish the quote then I'm afraid you're not in icon territory.
- Stay very up to date with Love of Huns.
- Don't waste your time settling for a partner who's not right for you in the hope you can change them. Icons never settle.

- Go into every given situation knowing that it's OK if you flash the nation. Look at Lateysha Grace who tried to twerk on *Big Brother's Bit on the Side* only for her dress to rip open and reveal her pink thong. Icon.
- Basically embody Gemma Collins – the GC is the icon of all icons. 'I'm claustrophobic, Darren.'

Over the years, while trying to figure out who I was and who I wanted to be, I've reinvented myself several times. When I first started out on social media, I was going for a wild, OTT, confrontational persona, basically someone who did not give a flying fuck. I wanted to be like the girls from *Geordie Shore* because I loved how they paved the way for excessive drinking, an example I followed as gospel. I also loved that they showed what dickheads men are and the way they refused to stand for their shit was sensational, so I'd channel Holly, Chloe, Vicky and Charlotte.

It was also a kind of self-preservation because I knew there would be people from school chatting shit about what I was doing online, sending the videos to each other, like, 'What the fuck is Grace doing? Hahahaha, this is so embarrassing for her.' So I felt I had to come across as if I really didn't care about them, even though I definitely did and still regularly stalked everyone on Facebook.

Identity crisis – how I've shapeshifted through the eras

School

ID: Shit-stirring gossiper

Characteristics: Desperate to get an ounce of attention from anyone, an embarrassing need to be liked.

College

ID: Wannabe nerd

Characteristics: A bit of confidence, a few opinions developed, able to make friends more easily, especially comfortable hanging out with geeks.

University

ID: Raver geezer bird

Characteristics: An accent like a London black cab driver to coincide with the start of GK Barry, out all the time, one of the lads.

Post-uni

ID: Essex girl

Characteristics: Still drunk and feral, always at a party and the person who would get that party going, more of a girls' girl than a ladette.

Now

ID: Boring old fart

Characteristics: Literally have to be paid to leave the house, being lazy is the default and where I'm happiest because quite frankly I ain't got the stamina these days. However, if at a bottomless brunch, you'd best believe I will reach for the tried-and-tested feral geezer bird identity and she's coming out to play.

GK Barry is like a more confident, extrovert and Cockney version of Grace. She's always one of the loudest people in the room, she's open and outrageous and doesn't mind who hears it, and I've definitely used that bolshy front to go into spaces I've not been sure about.

GK can be quite handy to hide behind when I need to.

Grace, on the other hand, is much more introverted. She'll still be the person working the room in a social situation but is happier to sit back and throw the occasional one-liner into a conversation rather than making herself the main character. She'd run off crying if anyone tried to start a fight.

Whereas GK is very sexual, Grace is a bit of a prude. Even though I talk about the gory details of my past situationships and hook-ups quite openly online, I'm actually really squeamish around that stuff and if Ella so much as tries to flirt with me, I'm like, 'Oh my God, stop,' because I get so embarrassed. I can't do a PDA. Even watching other people get it on together on *Love Island* makes me want to shrivel up and die.

As both GK Barry and Grace Keeling, I've spent the last couple of years flipping between two personalities, although they are gradually merging into one. At some point GK will be phased out because I'm not going to be still calling myself that when I'm 60, and also loads of people think I'm a goalkeeper called Barry so for the sake of my mental health, I'm going to have to revert to my actual name.

The real need to reach a happy medium came when I started getting booked for TV work and had to be more mainstream-friendly for a different audience, so I worked closely with a PR company who are still an integral part of my team and helped me walk that line. I didn't want to be sanitised to the point where I went from out-of-control dirtbag to advertising laundry detergent – I still wanted to be able to say what I thought and put it all out there, just in a way that allowed me to straddle (ahem) both versions of me.

Honestly, it took time to get right because, unintentionally, the PR training started to bleed into and influence what I was doing on the podcast. It was constantly in my head what I should and shouldn't say, but people listen to *Saving Grace* because they like the boundary-free, no-holds-barred, warts-and-all conversations. I found myself self-censoring and the chats suffered as a result.

It also impacted on what the team were cutting in the edit, especially after Bonnie Blue when everyone was freaking out about the backlash – the content deemed too near the knuckle meant I was being left with episodes that were about 15 minutes long.

We had to find a middle ground and so my genius solution was to get blackout drunk for the next podcast, say loads of crazy shit and then I felt a lot better for being back to my roots while my poor PR sat in the corner, beads of sweat forming on her forehead.

I have a lot of respect for my PR team and think we've just about pulled it off now. When I'm on telly, I'm still me but a calmer, safer version. To give you an example, we quite often cover the royal family on *Loose Women* and, with all due respect, I don't give a fuck about the royal family apart from Princess Anne who I'd love to get on the podcast because I think she's hardcore. If you're reading, Anne, DM me.

But other than her, I think they're all completely pointless which obviously I can't say on daytime ITV, so as a team we've found ways of expressing the fact I don't care about their lives without getting reported to Ofcom. I'll say that I'd like to see Princess Kate doing a mukbang or posting a couples' trend on TikTok – still kind of mocking them but not straying into territory that could be offensive.

It's a tightrope walk and I sometimes feel like I'm in the Houses of Parliament, representing an entire generation. I want more women my age and creators from TikTok to get hired but if I put a foot wrong then they'll use that to demonise the whole of Gen Z.

This is why I turn to drink.

What makes me unrelatable

- I buy cars that are so stupid I shouldn't be allowed by law on the road with them. I've currently got a pink Lamborghini and I've lived some of the best days of my life driving that car.
- I will fly business class every time. Even if the flight is one hour and the chairs are the same as economy with just a curtain between us, you'll find me at the front.
- Once when my flight was delayed and I was stuck at a Greek airport that was the definition of hell with no toilet seats, no soap and no doors on the cubicles, I googled 'private jets' and booked one to take me home. Not even sorry.
- Being able to take my dogs to any shoot because I'm the talent and talent gets a free pass on everything.
- Drinking on the job and having no one say anything because they think that's just GK Barry doing what she does.
- If I message a brand saying how much I love their stuff, they are sending me freebies.
- At Ella's football games, I'll usually be in a box which means I don't have to use the public toilets and that is everything to me.

- Never having to sit in a queue on a laptop trying to get tickets for concerts because a brand will usually take me.

After the jungle, when I started to move between the two identities more freely, it did cause some confusion. People thought this GK Barry character was a family-friendly, witty one-liner girl-next-door type who happened to be a lesbian because that's what they'd seen on *I'm a Celeb*. Oh fuck.

Obviously the jungle is edited in a very PG way – the reference to scissoring was as radical as it got and even then I'm sure there were plenty of people whose heads it still sailed over. Others might have had to google it and decided, 'Ah, right. I can see that scissoring's probably not for me.'

However, when I did the *Saving Grace: Jungle Fever* tour in 2025, lots of older women bought tickets on the back of seeing me on *I'm a Celeb* and I'm not joking, in every show I had pockets of the audience getting up and leaving halfway through because they'd thought they were coming to see the nice girl from the jungle. I'm not tarring all middle-aged women here – a lot of Boomers are the dirtiest people I know and make me look like the Virgin Mary – but I found it mortifying thinking these poor souls were going to go back home thinking I was an absolute disgrace.

There was always a certain point in the show that would tip them over the edge, guaranteeing a flurry of departures within a couple of minutes, and I'd know in my bones that it was coming. The sections where we, for example, discussed anal or various leaks from fannies were usually when Maureen from Macclesfield said, 'Yep, that's enough for me.'

Although what's arguably worse than that is when there's a 16-year-old sitting there flanked by their parents. I've seen dads with their daughters, looking at their kid going, 'What the fuck have you brought me to?' which is the most valid reaction ever. There was a time I couldn't even swear in front of my parents, so the thought of bringing them to a show with cock-shaped clouds firing confetti out the tips and talking about the clap would have finished all three of us off.

But they're used to it now and have become so desensitised/brainwashed that they even invite their friends along – on the last tour, my mum brought her gym instructor to a show that ended with a drag queen called Electra straddling and dry humping my dad in the front row. This unfortunate gym instructor guy was shellshocked afterwards. He was pale. I think he thought our whole family was on crack.

As an icon, I simply won't be participating in ...

- Dry January. Tried it, didn't make it, because who can do that in the most depressing month of the year?
- Any form of marathon.
- Dressing to please people, specifically men.

- Five fruit and veg a day. Who does that? My nan drank every day, I never saw her eat an apple and she lived until she was about 98.
- The 10,000 steps a day thing can GTF.
- Dancing on TikTok, although I fear I've fucked that one because I've started doing it on Ella's account. That's my version of flirting because she loves doing it so I'm like, 'Fuck it. Let's renegade.'
- Holding my tongue, I'm done with that. There are people in this world who need pulling up and it's OK to tell them that they need to stop being so insane.
- Doing a ball draw for the football. I'll probably count myself out of that in future.

Historically, I've been really bad at sticking up for myself, which is not the behaviour of an icon. I sometimes look back at past relationships and wish I'd felt more able to say 'fuck you' and then walk away. In jobs situations too, when I was first trying to get noticed, there were gigs where they would take the piss with what they would get me to do and how long I would work for because they knew that I wouldn't say no. I should have been able to say I didn't feel comfortable doing that, but I had a fear that pushing back would stop me from getting jobs in the future.

In this industry especially, I've found that men will try to embarrass you and make you feel small because they feel threatened by a woman coming in and doing the jobs they used to dominate. I've been on sets where the men won't take me seriously, or if I crack a joke, they'll say, 'Oh, I don't know if that's taking it too far,' when I know for a fact it wouldn't be an issue if a bloke had said it. Women are held to a different standard and we'd be flamed for coming out with some of the stuff that, for instance, Ricky Gervais says.

There's still this myth that women aren't funny and it's a stereotype that suits men for people to believe because it makes life easier for them. Funny women piss them off. Then they have to start that whole 'yeah, you're funny ... for a girl' routine.

I was recently doing some filming with a guy who happened to be an absolute prick. I'll spare his blushes here because he was so insignificant I can't actually remember his name or be bothered to google him.

He came in, sat down and said to me, 'You're the only funny girl on this show. The only one I'll actually laugh at.' Then he just started slating the other women, calling them tarts, and a few years ago I'd have awkwardly laughed along and then kicked myself later. But I wasn't having it this time.

I turned to him and said, 'You are morbidly obese, you look like you stink, and the absolute cheek of you to say all that about women when you actually need a mirror.'

And I watched him shrink, so I will be doing much more of this in the future.

If I was queen for the day I would ...

- Appoint women the head of everything and give all the shit jobs to the men.
- Put boob jobs and fanny tucks on the NHS because I think people would work harder if they felt good about themselves and therefore we'd increase our nation's productivity.
- Make Prosecco during work lunch breaks mandatory. Apart from anything else, we need to keep the economy of the pubs booming.
- Introduce a three-day working week so everyone is off from Thursday to Sunday.
- Declare an automatic national holiday whenever the sun comes out and order everyone to go to their nearest beer garden.
- Make it the law that everyone who has a baby must also take in a rescue dog or cat. An eye for an eye etc.
- Bring back that *Fat Families* show where the presenter is rude to everyone. Let's revive *Supernanny* as well. Basically,

all the problematic, shaming TV shows that have been cancelled because we can't cope with real talk. It would help people be way less touchy if all that shit was still on.

- Try and find a way of making men extinct.

I'm still a work in progress and probably always will be. I've accepted that I'm going to stumble my way through life, getting it right at some points and monumentally fucking it up at others. On regular occasions, both figuratively and literally, my tits are going to fall out for the world to see.

But what I am pretty sure of now is who I am and I'm locked in on staying true to that. Being unapologetically you means having the balls to show up as yourself, to say what you think, to set boundaries and to do all this without shame.

And that might mean that you're a bit all over the place, massively inconsistent and that you screw things up from time to time. But that is the whole point.

None of us should be trying to live our lives like a carefully curated, aesthetically pleasing Insta page or diluting who we are just to make other people feel comfortable. Own your strengths, weaknesses, best qualities and worst. That is being iconic.

My name is Grace and my toxic traits are ...

- I am an avid gossip but I also forget my sources. So someone will tell me, 'I've got this bit of tea, but just don't tell anyone.' About a week later I'll say to that same person, 'You'll never guess, I've got some unbelievable gossip for you … ' And they'll say, 'Yeah Grace, that's what I told you not to tell anyone.'
- Having no filter whatsoever and ending up talking to 90-year-old women about the fanny wax I had last week.
- Similarly, a steward who showed me where the loos were at Ella's football match said she couldn't believe I'd lasted the whole game without going. 'You need to do your Kegels, love,' I said to her. 'You must be flapping in the wind.' Then I had to apologise for being so inappropriate to this 60-year-old woman. Stuff like that keeps me up at night constantly.
- Assuming everyone agrees with my opinion and I won't back down. I have to be right and have that last word.
- Playing the victim card, especially in an argument which I'll try and win by making the other person feel sorry for me.
- Naming and shaming people on the podcast. I had Chloe Brockett on and told her I thought Jordan Brook was weird and such an ick, then I saw him and had to grovel.

- Goblin mode is my default. I wish I was a Sunday-reset-aesthetic clean girl, making an apple crumble at midday under soft lighting because what a lovely life they seem to be living, but the urge never lasts long because I'll have a bottle of wine, descend into savagery and ruin it all.

There is nothing I love more than when feral girls come up to me in the street to overshare their little hearts out and when they tell me about their STDs, outrageous nights out, prick boyfriends or the night they did a split on the dick during sex, I feel like a proud mother. That's my favourite.

So, my queens, Mummy says go forth and be cringe. Be loud, proud and *authentically* you. No filter, no shame, no worrying about what other people think. You are not a bit-part character, you're the whole entire main plot and this is your life. Fucking live it.

Your Dilemmas (Kind of) Solved

Dear Grace,

The other night I was out with some work friends. I'd only intended to stay for a couple but you know how it is – one drink led to another and when I was at the bar, getting in the latest round of Jägers, I happened to bump into my best friend's younger brother. We got chatting, the conversation turned a bit flirty and, to cut to the chase, before I knew it I'd taken him back to mine and shagged him senseless. Now I'm shitting myself that my friend will find out and it'll be the end of a ten-year friendship.

Should I get ahead of this and just tell her myself?

My queen. This actually happened to one of my friends at school so I do have some experience in this area and I would say, with all due respect, you have absolutely fucked it. The only thing you can do to save yourself is to take this with you to the grave and make sure you've blackmailed the brother so it never ever comes out. Because if it does, God help you. She's going to be proper fuming, she's not going to speak to you and she'll probably wish you a painful death for ever more.

Don't think that I'm judging you here because I've done some truly horrific things under the influence of drink, but take it as a really good lesson. Thou shalt not shag the brothers of best friends while pissed on Jägerbombs.

Dear Grace,

I've always been attracted to and have only ever dated boys and so assumed I was straight. However, I recently became friends with a girl I met at my reformer Pilates class and we've started going for a coffee after the sessions. She's funny, intelligent and really fucking hot. I've started to have feelings for her and I think she might feel the same. What should I do and am I now a lesbian?

Not to generalise, but the girls in my friendship group who have had crushes on their mates are all now raging lesbians. Having said that, sometimes with women, lines can get blurred because we're so similar and a close female friendship can feel like it might be something more. Especially if you've been fucked over by men. You don't need to put a label on something you're not sure of yet – I'd say there's a very fluid scale to all this and fancying your mate doesn't mean you have to go out, get an undercut, a septum piercing and start wearing jorts and sports bras.

I would recommend trying a little finger and seeing how you get on, no harm in that, although it might make your classes a bit awkward if you decide the muff is not for you after all. So be prepared to potentially have to find a new reformer Pilates class which shouldn't be hard because they are fucking everywhere.

Dear Grace,

My friend's dad has messaged me, having mistaken me for a prostitute, asking me for anal. How should I respond?

Ah, how wholesome. We've all been there, haven't we?

I honestly have so many follow-up questions here but let's get to the crux first. You can never tell your friend as it would ruin her life and she wouldn't be able to look her dad in the face again knowing he's a dirty perv who likes to take prostitutes up the arse. Because of this, I honestly think you need to distance yourself from her because if it was me, I'd be telling her after one glass of Prosecco. Change your number and move house if necessary.

As for how you should respond to the dad? Don't. No good can come of this.

Dear Grace,

I saw my next-door neighbour yesterday as I was putting the bins out and we stopped for a chat. I'm useless at small talk so I found all of this incredibly uncomfortable, which might explain why I accidentally said, 'Love you!' instead of 'See you later' as we parted ways. How can I ever leave the house again?

I feel you. I've said many dreadful things to delivery drivers, like the time one took a photo of the parcel and I said, 'Oh, you've got my feet in there – you owe me five quid.' He didn't laugh. He just left me hanging, probably thinking I was some sort of foot cam model, so I didn't answer the doors to deliveries for about three months after that.

Seriously, don't let this keep you awake at night. This level of embarrassment is small fry and you will do things that are far, far worse in your future. So take comfort from that cheery thought.

Dear Grace,

So, I'm madly in love with a new partner and we're planning on moving in together. The only snag is that she's allergic to dogs and I love them. I grew up with dogs and always imagined settling down with a partner and a load of pooches. Is this a dealbreaker?

If you're a lesbian, walk away now because this is not going to work out. Most lesbians have moved in after the first date and got a dog by the second, so either this relationship is no go or she's going to have to order in a truckload of Piriton and suck it up.

However, if you're straight, this is absolutely fine because you can just have a baby instead, which – if Noodle, Sherry-Baby and Kimchi are anything to go by – will be much easier than having a dog. A win-win.

Dear Grace,

I've been with this guy for about six months and he's quite an intense person to be in a relationship with. The main issue is his jealousy. He doesn't like me being friends with other men, he quizzes me about what's happened on nights out and he gets mad if he thinks a guy is looking at me. At first, it felt nice to be wanted and for someone to care about me, but now it's starting to feel suffocating. What should I do?

You are in for a horrific time if you stay with this prick. He's a walking, talking red flag who probably has a tiny penis and you need to get out of this immediately and be free. You must feel like a caged animal right now and so when you break it off, you're going to be euphoric. You're going to go wild and it will be the best time of your life. It will be BAFTA-winning levels of celebration. Run for the hills.

Dear Grace,

I've met this boy but have fallen in love with his brother and we ended up having a three-way. Now what?

I don't really know what your dilemma is, hun. Are you distraught about what the fuck you've done? Because I mean this in the nicest possible way but there's no way you're going to be able to stay with either of the brothers after this, so the best thing to do would be to pack your bags and move to Switzerland. These men are not for you.

Also, can I just query why these brothers are getting into bed together? I actually know twin sisters who will shag guys at the same time and that to me is mental. If you had a gun to my head and said that in order not to die, I had to sleep with someone along with my brother, I would choose death. If that was my only choice, I would absolutely be more than happy to take the bullet and go in that moment.

Dear Grace,

I'm friends with a couple who have recently got engaged. The only thing is, he's told me that the only reason he's marrying her is because she's 'the safe option'. What should I do? Tell his fiancée the awful truth or just stay out of it?

As soon as I know a person is cheating or anything like that, I'm someone who will tell the partner even if it's none of my business. I make it my business because I know I'd want someone to tell me. So, if this was me in your position, I'd pluck up the courage to break the bad news to her but be aware that you'll likely need some proof before you drop a bomb like that. Get him to say it again and secretly record it (what could possibly go wrong here?) because otherwise he's going to deny it and you'll look like a drama starter.

See it this way, if they go ahead and get married, this marriage is definitely not going to work out and divorces are expensive, so you'd be saving this poor cow from financial ruin. If she still goes ahead and marries him anyway, at least you've got that guilt off your shoulders.

Dear Grace,

I'm in the middle of a big decision – whether or not to move in with my girlfriend. I love her and want a future together but I'm not a fan of her kids and unfortunately they come as part of the deal. What do you think I should do?

If you don't like her kids, you shouldn't be with her. Even if the kids are older, with the state of the cozzie livs, they're not going to be moving out anytime soon. Why are you dating someone with kids anyway? If you hate children so much, maybe date someone who doesn't have any. And, by the way, I hear you. I would never be with someone who has kids purely because most children are arseholes and I'd be an awful stepmum.

Dear Grace,

I'm a lesbian and have been casually seeing two girls and I genuinely like them both the same. I know I need to make a choice but I can't decide. How can I work out which one to stay with?

Easy. I would do a pros and cons list of their qualities and flaws. One might have a juicy arse (pro) but not brush her teeth at night (con). These are all things you have to consider when choosing a life partner. Think about which one you would prefer to live with when you're older – when you retire and you have to be with that person 24/7, you need someone who is going to make you laugh. That should be the priority because that arse ain't going to be so juicy at 90.

A Letter to My 16-Year-Old Self

Dearest queen,

What can I tell you? Well, I'm ten years further down the line and so the answer to that is quite a fucking lot. And I swear, most of the news is all right.

But let's start with the not quite so good and get that out the way first.

Sorry to break it to you, but you're still going to be struggling with the whole flat arse thing. That bitch won't grow. You're also still going to have the acne, I'm afraid. Yep, I completely agree – that's shit and you should definitely sue.

However, on the plus side I can reveal that you have a tiny bit more tit and I'm sure you'll be happy to know that you're still a skinny legend.

Everything you think is going to be life-ending now won't be. It doesn't even matter that you fail nearly all of your GCSEs – your teachers and parents majorly overdid the seriousness of that. In fact, you'll make it to uni and come out with an actual degree. Neither is it important that you don't have a solid group of friends just now because you're about to go to college and then uni after that and I promise you're going to be flooded with mates. School is not the be all and end all. You will never hear from the populars again which, believe me, is incredible news for you.

I know you care a hell of a lot about what others think of you and that's not really going to change, but you will reach a point where it doesn't affect you quite as much. Just know that the people whose opinions you stress over at the moment don't stay in your life so they're really not worth getting your knickers in a knot about.

You probably need to calm down and stop chasing boys. Boys at 16 are not in any way hygienic – they don't even wash their legs and they should be avoided at all costs. There is no need to be in a relationship for the sake of it, despite what you might think right now.

While we're on this topic, there are a few breakups ahead of you, but you will take a lot from them and they are all leading you somewhere so amazing you can't even imagine. Honestly, if I told you, you'd think I was taking the piss and it might even make you feel slightly unwell. Put it this way, there's a great big vagina-shaped curveball heading in your direction and, trust me here, it's going to be the most epic thing to ever happen to you.

Life is going to take you on some mental twists and turns and if I was to list them all here, some of them would blow your mind. You know that chronic fear of flying? Not only will you overcome it, you will do so while being flown to Australia to take part in a TV show you've loved and watched your whole life. Not even joking.

Your emetophobia is going to get significantly worse before it gets better and you're going to be in a world of bother for a while, but you do come out the other side of it. And you will discover an anti-travel sickness tablet that is going to change everything.

Embrace all of the (many) mistakes you're about to make. They're going to be very stressful at the time but one day they'll make really funny stories for TikTok.

What's TikTok? Lol. That's a very good question. Basically, you know that shit app called Musical.ly? Yeah, don't bother with that, but do pay close attention because it will soon turn into something else and that thing is going to make you lots of money. So go ahead and date that drug dealer, live in a hostel and even get yourself a dose of chlamydia cos it's all great content for the future.

Apologies in advance but I will one day announce on national television that you used to watch emo boys kissing on YouTube. I know that's your darkest secret right now, but you'll be glad to know that you've grown out of it by the age of 26 and I have even confirmed with other people since that it's a semi-normal thing to do. You're not the freak you think you are.

The best bit of advice I can give you is to slow down and stop trying to grow up too quickly because – and I know this is a cliché – life goes so fast. Take your time and be a bit kinder to yourself because everything you're losing sleep over now will work out in the end.

Finally, try not to give your mum such a hard time because she's actually a legend who loves you to pieces and in a few years' time she's going to become one of your best mates.

I'm not going to pretend that everything in your mid-twenties is magically perfect. You're not going to have it all figured out; things remain a bit messy and you're still capable of making truly terrible decisions. But you are a lot happier in yourself. You have great people around you and life is pretty sweet overall.

So carry on as you are, babe. You're going to be fine.

Love from,

Grace

x x x

P.S. Get rid of those bleached-blonde slag strips at the front of your hair. They are fucking hideous.

ACKNOWLEDGEMENTS

Firstly, thank you to every single person who has followed me throughout the years, especially when I had my soap brows (IYKYK). Your loyalty to me never goes unnoticed and I love that we are all a bit weird together.

I want to thank my manager Hannah who took a chance on me and has taken me to incredible heights while always believing in me. She has constantly fought my corner in rooms that I'm not in and she also made being ginger cool again so I really can't fault her.

Thank you to my parents for raising me with so much love and for always believing in me. Whenever I'd tell them I was too stupid to do something, they would always tell me I could do it and I always did. They have also kept me painfully humble as they like to remind me that I used to be a massive-headed, gravestone-toothed girl, and just because I'm on *Loose Women* it doesn't take away from the fact I used to piss the bed till a late age – God bless.

Thanks also to Beth for helping me put all these stories into this book and for making them make sense while bringing so much fun to the whole process. That poor woman will be needing to see a therapist after everything I've divulged.

Lastly, I want to thank my girlfriend Ella for always being so supportive of everything I do and giving me a space where I can completely be myself. She's had to listen to hours of me being anxious and having menty bs and she only ever gives me support throughout. I'd also like to thank her for turning me into a raging lez – what a day to be gay. x